PHP AND MYSQL

BUILDING EFFICIENT AND SECURE
APPLICATION

OLIVER LUCAS JR

Copyright © 2024 by Oliver Lucas Jr

All rights reserved. No part of this publication may be reproduced, distributed, or transmitted in any form or by any means, including photocopying, recording, or other electronic or mechanical methods, without the prior written permission of the publisher, except in the case of brief quotations embodied in critical reviews and certain other non commercial uses permitted by copyright law.

9. Test Your Environment

Create a PHP file: Create a file named `index.php` in your web server's root directory (e.g., `/var/www/html` on Linux, `htdocs` in XAMPP).

Add PHP code: Add the following code to `index.php`:

PHP

```php
<?php
    phpinfo();
?>
```

Access in browser: Open a web browser and go to `http://localhost/index.php`. You should see the PHP information page, indicating that PHP is working correctly.

10. Connect to MySQL

Command Line: Use the MySQL command-line client to connect to your MySQL server.

PHP: Use PHP code to connect to MySQL and execute queries:

PHP

```php
<?php
$servername = "localhost";
$username = "your_username";
$password = "your_password";
$dbname = "your_database";

// Create connection
$conn = new mysqli($servername, $username, $password, $dbname);
```

```php
// Check connection
if ($conn->connect_error)[1] {
        die("Connection        failed:       "       .
$conn->connect_error);
}
echo "Connected successfully";[2]
?>
```

By following these steps, you'll have a fully functional development environment ready for building your PHP and MySQL applications. Remember to consult the documentation for each component for detailed installation and configuration instructions.

2.2 Control structures (if/else, loops).

Control structures are the building blocks of programming logic. They allow you to control the flow of execution in your PHP code, making it possible to create dynamic and interactive applications. Here's a breakdown of the key control structures in PHP:

1. Conditional Statements

Conditional statements let you execute different blocks of code based on whether a condition is true or false.

if **statement:** Executes a block of code if a condition is true.

PHP

```php
<?php
$age = 20;

if ($age >= 18) {
  echo "You are an adult.";
}
```

```
?>
```

if...else **statement:** Executes one block of code if a condition is true, and another block if it's false.

PHP

```php
<?php
$age = 15;

if ($age >= 18) {
  echo "You are an adult.";
} else {
  echo "You are a minor.";
}
?>
```

if...elseif...else **statement:** Allows you to check multiple conditions sequentially.

PHP

```php
<?php
$grade = 85;

if ($grade >= 90) {
  echo "You got an A!";
} elseif ($grade >= 80) {
  echo "You got a B!";
} elseif ($grade >= 70) {
  echo "You got a C.";
} else {
  echo "You need to study harder.";
```

```
}
?>
```

switch **statement:** Provides a way to compare a variable against multiple values.

PHP

```php
<?php
$day = "Monday";

switch ($day) {
  case "Monday":
    echo "It's the start of the week.";
    break;
  case "Friday":
    echo "It's almost the weekend!";
    break;
  default:
    echo "It's a regular[1] weekday.";
}
?>
```

2. Loops

Loops allow you to execute a block of code repeatedly.

for **loop:** Repeats a block of code a specific number of times.

PHP

```php
<?php
for ($i = 0; $i < 5; $i++) {
  echo "Iteration: " . $i . "<br>";
```

```
}
?>
```

while **loop:** Repeats a block of code as long as a condition is true.

PHP

```php
<?php
$count = 0;
while ($count < 5) {
    echo "Count: " . $count . "<br>";
    $count++;
}
?>
```

do...while **loop:** Similar to a while loop, but the code block is executed at least once, even if the condition is initially false.[2]

PHP

```php
<?php
$count = 0;
do {
    echo "Count: " . $count . "<br>";
    $count++;
} while ($count < 5);
?>
```

foreach **loop:** Used to iterate over arrays.

PHP

```php
<?php
$colors = array("red", "green", "blue");

foreach ($colors as $color) {
  echo $color . "<br>";
}
?>
```

Important Loop Control Statements:

`break`: Exits the current loop.

`continue`: Skips the current Iteration and continues to the next.

By understanding and using these control structures, you can create complex logic and dynamic behavior in your PHP applications. They are essential for handling user input, processing data, and making decisions based on different conditions.

2.3 Functions and arrays.

Functions

Functions are reusable blocks of code that perform specific tasks. They help you organize your code, make it more modular, and avoid repetition. Here's how they work in PHP:

Defining a function:

PHP

```php
<?php
function greet($name) {
  echo "Hello, " . $name . "!";
}
?>
```

Calling a function:

PHP

```php
<?php
greet("Alice"); // Outputs: Hello, Alice!
?>
```

Returning values:

PHP

```php
<?php
function add($num1, $num2) {
  return $num1 + $num2;
}

$result = add(5, 3); // $result will be 8
?>
```

Function arguments:

PHP

```php
<?php
function greet($name = "World") {  // Default argument
  echo "Hello, " . $name . "!";
}

greet(); // Outputs: Hello, World!
greet("Bob"); // Outputs: Hello, Bob!
```

```php
?>
```

Arrays

Arrays are data structures that allow you to store multiple values in a single variable. They are incredibly useful for organizing and manipulating collections of data.

Creating an array:

PHP

```php
<?php
$colors = array("red", "green", "blue");
// or
$colors = ["red", "green", "blue"]; // Short
array syntax
?>
```

Accessing array elements:

PHP

```php
<?php
echo $colors[0]; // Outputs: red
?>
```

Associative arrays:

PHP

```php
<?php
$person = array("name" => "Alice", "age" => 30);
```

TABLE OF CONTENTS

Chapter 8

Chapter 9

Chapter 10

Chapter 11

Chapter 12

Preface

"! This book is your comprehensive guide to mastering PHP and MySQL and building efficient, secure, and dynamic web applications. Whether you're a beginner taking your first steps into web development or an experienced programmer looking to expand your skillset, this book will equip you with the knowledge and practical techniques you need to succeed.

Why PHP and MySQL?

PHP and MySQL are a powerful combination for web development. PHP, a versatile scripting language, seamlessly integrates with HTML to create dynamic web pages. MySQL, a robust and reliable database system, provides a solid foundation for storing and managing your application's data. Together, they form a cornerstone of the web, powering countless websites and applications, from small personal blogs to large-scale enterprise systems.

What You'll Learn

This book takes a practical, hands-on approach to learning PHP and MySQL. You'll start with the fundamentals, covering the basics of both technologies and setting up your development environment. Then, you'll dive into building real-world applications, exploring topics like:

Database design and interaction: Mastering SQL and building efficient database structures.

Security: Protecting your applications from common threats like SQL injection and cross-site scripting.

Efficiency: Optimizing your code and database queries for performance.

User authentication and session management: Implementing secure login and registration systems.

Dynamic content: Creating web pages that respond to user input and data changes.

Advanced topics: Building RESTful APIs, working with caching techniques, and scaling your applications.

Who This Book Is For

This book is for anyone who wants to learn PHP and MySQL web development. Whether you're a:

Beginner: Starting your web development journey.

Student: Learning web development in a classroom setting.

Hobbyist: Building websites and applications for personal projects.

Professional: Expanding your skills and taking your career to the next level.

How to Use This Book

This book is designed to be read sequentially, but you can also use it as a reference guide for specific topics. Each chapter builds upon the previous ones, introducing new concepts and techniques. Code examples are provided throughout the book, allowing you to experiment and apply what you learn.

Your Journey Begins

We're excited to guide you on your journey to becoming a proficient PHP and MySQL developer. With dedication and practice, you'll be able to build dynamic, secure, and efficient web applications that meet the demands of the modern web.

Let's get started!

Chapter 1

Why PHP and MySQL?

1.1 A brief history of PHP and MySQL.

PHP

Early Days (1994): Rasmus Lerdorf created PHP Tools, a simple set of scripts to track visits to his online resume. This was the very beginning of PHP!

PHP/FI (1995): Lerdorf expanded his tools, adding form handling and database interaction, calling it "Personal Home Page/Forms Interpreter" (PHP/FI).

PHP 3 (1997): Andi Gutmans and Zeev Suraski completely rewrote the parser, laying the foundation for modern PHP. The name changed to the recursive acronym "PHP: Hypertext Preprocessor." This version saw a surge in popularity.

PHP 4 (2000): Introduced the Zend Engine, significantly improving performance. This era saw PHP become a dominant language for web development.

PHP 5 (2004): Major improvements to object-oriented programming and introduced new features like exceptions and XML support.

PHP 7 (2015): A huge leap forward with significant performance enhancements, making PHP even faster and more efficient.

PHP 8 (2020): Continued the focus on performance and added features like the JIT compiler, attributes, and union types.

MySQL

Early Development (1995): Michael Widenius, David Axmark, and Allan Larsson at MySQL AB began developing MySQL, aiming for a fast and reliable database system.

Open Source Release (2000): MySQL went open source, making it accessible to a wider audience and contributing to its rapid adoption.

Acquisition by Sun Microsystems (2008): Sun acquired MySQL AB, further solidifying its position in the market.

Acquisition by Oracle (2010): Oracle acquired Sun, and with it, MySQL. This led to some concerns in the open-source community, but MySQL remains a popular choice.

Continued Development: MySQL continues to be actively developed, with new versions offering improved performance, security, and features.

PHP and MySQL: A Powerful Duo

PHP and MySQL have a long history of working together. They are often used together in the LAMP stack (Linux, Apache, MySQL, PHP), a popular open-source web development platform. This combination has powered countless websites and applications over the years.

Both PHP and MySQL have evolved significantly over time, adapting to the changing needs of the web. They remain popular choices for web development due to their ease of use, flexibility, and strong community support.

1.2 The LAMP stack and its advantages.

The LAMP stack is a popular open-source software bundle used for web development.[1] It's an acronym that stands for:

Linux: The operating system.[2]

Apache: The web server software.[3]

MySQL: The database management system.[4]

PHP: The scripting language.[5]

Here's a breakdown of the components and why they work so well together:

Linux: A stable and secure operating system that provides the foundation for the stack.[6] It's known for its reliability and flexibility, making it a great choice for web servers.[7]

Apache: A powerful and widely-used web server that handles HTTP requests and serves web pages.[8] It's highly configurable and can be extended with modules to support various functionalities.[9]

MySQL: A robust and efficient relational database management system.[10] It's used to store and manage the data for your web applications.[11]

PHP: A server-side scripting language specifically designed for web development.[12] It's embedded within HTML code and used to generate dynamic content.[13]

Advantages of the LAMP Stack:

Cost-effective: All the components are open-source and free to use, which significantly reduces development costs.[14]

Flexibility: Each component can be replaced or customized to meet specific project requirements.[15] For example, you could swap MySQL for PostgreSQL or MariaDB.[16]

Performance: The LAMP stack is known for its good performance, especially when properly configured and optimized.[17]

Security: Linux is inherently secure, and the other components have a strong track record of security updates and patches.[18]

Community Support: A large and active community supports the LAMP stack, providing ample resources, documentation, and assistance.[19]

Ease of Deployment: Setting up a LAMP environment is relatively straightforward, with many hosting providers offering one-click installations.[20]

Cross-Platform Compatibility: While "L" stands for Linux, the stack can also be installed on other operating systems like Windows (WAMP) and macOS (MAMP).[21]

Scalability: LAMP applications can be easily scaled to handle increased traffic and data loads.[22]

Why is it so popular?

The LAMP stack's popularity stems from its combination of power, flexibility, and affordability.[23] It's a mature and reliable platform that has been used to build countless websites and web applications, from small personal blogs to large-scale enterprise systems.[24] Its open-source nature encourages collaboration and innovation, making it a favorite among developers worldwide.[25]

1.3 Use cases for PHP and MySQL (web applications, e-commerce, content management systems).

PHP and MySQL are a powerful combination for web development, offering flexibility and robustness for a wide range of applications.[1] Here are some of their common use cases:

1. Web Applications

Dynamic Websites: PHP allows you to create dynamic web pages that respond to user input and display customized content.[2] This is essential for interactive websites, user dashboards, and personalized experiences.[3]

Custom Applications: PHP and MySQL can be used to build a wide variety of web applications tailored to specific business needs, such as CRM systems, project management tools, and internal collaboration platforms.[4]

Data-Driven Applications: MySQL provides a reliable way to store and manage data, while PHP allows you to access and manipulate that data to create dynamic and interactive features.[5]

2. E-commerce

Online Stores: PHP and MySQL are the foundation of many popular e-commerce platforms.[6] MySQL stores product information, customer data, and orders, while PHP handles user interactions, shopping carts, and payment processing.[7]

Product Catalogs: Dynamically generate and manage product catalogs with features like filtering, sorting, and searching.[8]

Order Management: Process orders, track shipments, and manage customer interactions.[9]

Secure Transactions: Implement secure payment gateways and protect sensitive customer data.[10]

3. Content Management Systems (CMS)

Websites and Blogs: PHP and MySQL power popular CMS platforms like WordPress, Drupal, and Joomla.[11] These systems make it easy to create and manage websites without extensive coding knowledge.[12]

Custom CMS Solutions: Develop tailored CMS solutions for specific content management needs, such as news websites, online magazines, or corporate intranets.[13]

Content Creation and Editing: Provide user-friendly interfaces for creating, editing, and publishing content.[14]

User Management: Manage user roles, permissions, and access to content.[15]

4. Other Use Cases

Social Networking Platforms: PHP can handle the real-time interactions and data processing required for social networking features.[16]

Data Analytics and Reporting: PHP can be used to generate reports and analyze data stored in MySQL.[17]

Email Marketing: PHP can be used to create and send email campaigns, manage mailing lists, and track email marketing performance.[18]

Why PHP and MySQL are a good fit:

Ease of Use: PHP is relatively easy to learn and use, making it a good choice for beginners.[19] MySQL is also user-friendly and offers a straightforward way to manage data.[20]

Flexibility: PHP and MySQL can be used to build a wide range of applications, from simple websites to complex enterprise systems.[21]

Performance: Both PHP and MySQL are known for their good performance, especially when optimized correctly.

Scalability: PHP and MySQL applications can be scaled to handle increasing traffic and data loads.[22]

Strong Community Support: A large and active community supports both technologies, offering ample resources, documentation, and assistance.[23]

This versatility and wide range of applications make PHP and MySQL a popular choice for web development projects of all sizes.

1.4 Setting up your development environment.

Setting up your development environment is the first step to building PHP and MySQL applications. Here's a guide to get you started:

1. Choose Your Operating System

Linux: A popular choice for web development due to its stability, security, and open-source nature. Distributions like Ubuntu, Debian, and Fedora are commonly used.

macOS: Provides a Unix-based environment and comes with pre-installed tools like Apache and PHP.

Windows: You can use WAMP (Windows, Apache, MySQL, PHP) packages to simplify the installation process on Windows.

2. Install a Web Server

Apache: The most popular web server, known for its reliability and flexibility.

Nginx: A lightweight and high-performance alternative to Apache.

3. Install PHP

Download from PHP.net: Download the latest version of PHP from the official website.

Package Managers: Use your operating system's package manager (e.g., `apt` on Ubuntu, `brew` on macOS) to install PHP.

4. Install MySQL

Download from MySQL.com: Download the MySQL Community Server.

Package Managers: Use your package manager to install MySQL.

5. Install a Text Editor or IDE

Text Editors: Sublime Text, Atom, VS Code (with PHP extensions) are lightweight and good for beginners.

IDEs: PhpStorm, NetBeans provide advanced features like code completion, debugging, and refactoring tools.

6. (Optional) Install a Local Development Environment

XAMPP: A cross-platform package that includes Apache, MariaDB (a MySQL fork), PHP, and Perl.

WAMP: A Windows-specific package with Apache, MySQL, and PHP.

MAMP: A macOS-specific package with Apache, MySQL, and PHP.

Docker: Containerizes your application and its dependencies, ensuring consistency across different environments.

7. Configure PHP

php.ini: Locate and edit the `php.ini` file to configure PHP settings like error reporting, file uploads, and extensions.

8. Configure MySQL

MySQL Configuration File: Configure MySQL settings like port number, user accounts, and database directories.

9. Test Your Environment

Create a PHP file: Create a file named `index.php` in your web server's root directory (e.g., `/var/www/html` on Linux, `htdocs` in XAMPP).

Add PHP code: Add the following code to `index.php`:

PHP

```php
<?php
    phpinfo();
?>
```

Access in browser: Open a web browser and go to `http://localhost/index.php`. You should see the PHP information page, indicating that PHP is working correctly.

10. Connect to MySQL

Command Line: Use the MySQL command-line client to connect to your MySQL server.

PHP: Use PHP code to connect to MySQL and execute queries:

PHP

```php
<?php
$servername = "localhost";
$username = "your_username";
$password = "your_password";
$dbname = "your_database";
```

```php
// Create connection
$conn  =  new  mysqli($servername,  $username,
$password, $dbname);

// Check connection
if ($conn->connect_error)[1] {
        die("Connection       failed:       "       .
$conn->connect_error);
}
echo "Connected successfully";[2]
?>
```

By following these steps, you'll have a fully functional development environment ready for building your PHP and MySQL applications. Remember to consult the documentation for each component for detailed installation and configuration instructions.

Chapter 2

PHP Fundamentals

2.1 Basic syntax, variables, data types.

Setting up your development environment is the first step to building PHP and MySQL applications. Here's a guide to get you started:

1. Choose Your Operating System

Linux: A popular choice for web development due to its stability, security, and open-source nature. Distributions like Ubuntu, Debian, and Fedora are commonly used.

macOS: Provides a Unix-based environment and comes with pre-installed tools like Apache and PHP.

Windows: You can use WAMP (Windows, Apache, MySQL, PHP) packages to simplify the installation process on Windows.

2. Install a Web Server

Apache: The most popular web server, known for its reliability and flexibility.

Nginx: A lightweight and high-performance alternative to Apache.

3. Install PHP

Download from PHP.net: Download the latest version of PHP from the official website.

Package Managers: Use your operating system's package manager (e.g., `apt` on Ubuntu, `brew` on macOS) to install PHP.

4. Install MySQL

Download from MySQL.com: Download the MySQL Community Server.

Package Managers: Use your package manager to install MySQL.

5. Install a Text Editor or IDE

Text Editors: Sublime Text, Atom, VS Code (with PHP extensions) are lightweight and good for beginners.

IDEs: PhpStorm, NetBeans provide advanced features like code completion, debugging, and refactoring tools.

6. (Optional) Install a Local Development Environment

XAMPP: A cross-platform package that includes Apache, MariaDB (a MySQL fork), PHP, and Perl.

WAMP: A Windows-specific package with Apache, MySQL, and PHP.

MAMP: A macOS-specific package with Apache, MySQL, and PHP.

Docker: Containerizes your application and its dependencies, ensuring consistency across different environments.

7. Configure PHP

php.ini: Locate and edit the `php.ini` file to configure PHP settings like error reporting, file uploads, and extensions.

8. Configure MySQL

MySQL Configuration File: Configure MySQL settings like port number, user accounts, and database directories.

```
// or
$person = ["name" => "Alice", "age" => 30];

echo $person["name"]; // Outputs: Alice
?>
```

Multidimensional arrays:

PHP

```
<?php
$matrix = array(
   array(1, 2, 3),
   array(4, 5, 6),
   array(7, 8, 9)
);

echo $matrix[1][2]; // Outputs: 6
?>
```

Useful Array Functions

PHP provides many built-in functions for working with arrays:

`count($array)`: Returns the number of elements in an array.

`sort($array)`: Sorts the elements of an array.

`array_push($array, $value)`: Adds an element to the end of an array.

`array_pop($array)`: Removes the last element from an array.

`array_merge($array1, $array2)`: Merges two or more arrays.

`array_keys($array)`: Returns all the keys of an array.

`array_values($array)`: Returns all the values of an array.

Combining Functions and Arrays

Functions and arrays often work together. You can pass arrays as arguments to functions, and functions can return arrays. This allows you to create powerful and flexible code for processing collections of data.

PHP

```php
<?php
function printArray($array) {
  foreach ($array as $value) {
    echo $value . " ";
  }
  echo "<br>";
}

$numbers = [1, 2, 3, 4, 5];
printArray($numbers); // Outputs: 1 2 3 4 5
?>
```

By mastering functions and arrays, you'll be well-equipped to write efficient and organized PHP code for a wide range of applications.

2.4 Object-oriented programming in PHP.

Object-oriented programming (OOP) is a powerful paradigm that allows you to structure your code around "objects," which combine data (properties) and actions (methods) that operate on that data. This approach brings many benefits to PHP development, including:

Key Concepts in OOP:

Classes: Blueprints for creating objects. They define the properties (variables) and methods (functions) that objects of that class will have.

Objects: Instances of a class. Each object has its own set of properties and can access the methods defined in its class.

Properties: Variables that hold data within an object.

Methods: Functions that define the behavior of an object.

Encapsulation: Bundling data and methods that operate on that data within a class, protecting the data from unauthorized access.

Inheritance: Creating new classes (child classes) that inherit properties and methods from existing classes (parent classes).

Polymorphism: The ability of different objects to respond to the same method call in their own way.

Abstraction: Simplifying complex systems by hiding unnecessary details and presenting only essential information.

Example of OOP in PHP:

PHP

```php
<?php
// Define a class called "Car"
class Car {
  // Properties
  public $make;
  public $model;
  public $year;

  // Constructor method
    public function __construct($make, $model, $year) {
    $this->make = $make;
```

```php
    $this->model = $model;
    $this->year = $year;
  }

  // Method to display car information
  public function displayInfo() {
    echo "Make: " . $this->make . "<br>";
    echo "Model: " . $this->model . "<br>";
    echo "Year: " . $this->year . "<br>";
  }
}

// Create an object of the Car class
$myCar = new Car("Toyota", "Camry", 2023);

// Call the displayInfo method
$myCar->displayInfo();
 ?>
```

Benefits of OOP in PHP:

Modularity: Code is organized into reusable classes, making it easier to maintain and update.

Reusability: Classes and objects can be reused in different parts of an application or even in other projects.

Flexibility: Inheritance and polymorphism allow you to create flexible and adaptable code.

Maintainability: OOP code is generally easier to understand and debug.

Scalability: OOP makes it easier to build complex and large-scale applications.

When to Use OOP in PHP:

Complex Applications: When building applications with many interacting components and complex logic.

Code Reusability: When you need to reuse code in different parts of your application or across multiple projects.

Large Projects: When working on projects with a team of developers, OOP helps with code organization and collaboration.

By understanding and applying the principles of OOP, you can write more efficient, maintainable, and scalable PHP code.

Chapter 3

Introduction to Databases and MySQL

3.1 Relational Databases

Imagine a well-organized spreadsheet. That's the basic idea behind a relational database. It stores data in tables with rows and columns, just like a spreadsheet. But it takes it a step further:

Tables: Each table holds a specific type of data (e.g., a "customers" table, a "products" table).

Columns: Columns define the attributes of the data (e.g., "customer_id," "name," "email" in the "customers" table).

Rows: Each row represents a single record (e.g., information about one specific customer).

Relationships: The "relational" part comes in when you connect tables based on related data. For example, you might link the "customers" table to an "orders" table using a "customer_id" column that exists in both tables.

Why use relational databases?

Organized Data: Data is structured and easy to access.

Data Integrity: Rules and constraints ensure data accuracy and consistency.

Efficiency: Efficient for storing and retrieving large amounts of structured data.

Flexibility: Can easily handle changes to your data structure.

Reduced Redundancy: By linking tables, you avoid storing the same data multiple times.

SQL (Structured Query Language)

SQL is the language you use to talk to relational databases. It's like a set of commands for managing and manipulating data. Here are some common SQL commands:

`SELECT`: Retrieves data from a table.

Example: `SELECT name, email FROM customers;`

`INSERT`: Adds new data to a table.

Example: `INSERT INTO customers (name, email) VALUES ('John Doe', 'john@example.com');`

`UPDATE`: Modifies existing data in a table.

Example: `UPDATE customers SET email = 'newemail@example.com' WHERE customer_id = 1;`

`DELETE`: Removes data from a table.

Example: `DELETE FROM customers WHERE customer_id = 1;`

`CREATE TABLE`: Creates a new table in the database.

`ALTER TABLE`: Modifies the structure of an existing table.

`DROP TABLE`: Deletes a table from the database.[1]

SQL is essential for:

Creating and managing databases.

Storing, retrieving, and updating data.

Defining relationships between tables.

Controlling access to data.

Ensuring data integrity.

Popular Relational Database Management Systems (RDBMS)

MySQL: Open-source, widely used, and known for its performance.

PostgreSQL: Powerful open-source database with advanced features.

Oracle Database: A commercial database system often used in enterprise applications.

Microsoft SQL Server: A commercial database system from Microsoft.

SQLite: A lightweight database often embedded in applications.

Relational databases and SQL are fundamental to many web applications. They provide a robust and efficient way to store and manage the data that powers dynamic websites, e-commerce platforms, and content management systems.

3.2 Installing and configuring MySQL.

1. Download MySQL

Go to the source: Visit the official MySQL website (mysql.com) and navigate to the downloads section.

Community Server: Choose the "MySQL Community Server" edition – it's free and open source.

Select your OS: You'll find installers for Windows, macOS, and Linux. Choose the one that matches your system.

Linux variations: Linux distributions often have their own ways of packaging MySQL. You might find it easier to use your distribution's package manager (like `apt` on Debian/Ubuntu or `yum` on Fedora/CentOS).

2. Installation

Windows:

Run the downloaded `.msi` installer.

Select the "Developer Default" setup type (this is usually the best option for development).

Follow the on-screen prompts. You'll be asked to set a root password – **make this a strong password!**

macOS:

Open the downloaded `.dmg` file and run the installer.

Follow the instructions and set a root password.

You might need to add the MySQL bin directory to your system's PATH environment variable, so you can easily access MySQL commands from the terminal.

Linux:

If you're using a package manager:

Update your package list (e.g., `sudo apt-get update`).

Install the MySQL server package (e.g., `sudo apt-get install mysql-server`).

If you're using the downloaded installer, follow the instructions provided.

You'll be prompted to set a root password during the installation.

3. Configuration

Configuration file: MySQL uses a configuration file to store its settings. This file is usually named `my.cnf` (Linux) or `my.ini` (Windows). You can find it in the MySQL installation directory.

Key settings:

`port`: The port MySQL listens on (default is 3306).

`datadir`: The directory where MySQL stores your databases.

`bind-address`: The IP address MySQL listens on (usually 127.0.0.1 for local access only).

Security:

Strong root password: Essential for protecting your server.

Remove anonymous users: MySQL might come with anonymous user accounts. It's best to remove these.

Restrict root access: Configure MySQL to only allow root login from the local machine (`localhost` or `127.0.0.1`).

4. Verification

Connect to the server:

Command line: Open your terminal or command prompt and use the `mysql` client:

Bash

```
mysql -u root -p
```

Enter your root password when prompted.

GUI tools: If you prefer a visual interface, you can use tools like MySQL Workbench or phpMyAdmin to connect to your server.

Important Notes:

Security first: Always prioritize security when setting up your MySQL server. Use strong passwords, keep your server software updated, and follow security best practices.

Backups are essential: Regularly back up your databases to prevent data loss.

Read the documentation: The official MySQL documentation is an invaluable resource. Refer to it for detailed instructions specific to your OS and MySQL version.

3.3 Basic SQL commands (SELECT, INSERT, UPDATE, DELETE).

SQL (Structured Query Language) is what you use to communicate with your MySQL database. Here's a breakdown of the essential commands:

1. SELECT (Retrieve data)

The SELECT statement is used to retrieve data from one or more tables.

Basic syntax:

SQL

```
SELECT column1, column2, ...
FROM table_name;
```

Example: Retrieve the `name` and `email` from a table called `customers`:

SQL

```
SELECT name, email
 FROM customers;
```

Selecting all columns: Use * to select all columns:

SQL

```
SELECT * FROM customers;
```

Filtering data with `WHERE`:

SQL

```
SELECT *
 FROM customers
WHERE country = 'USA';
```

Sorting data with `ORDER BY`:

SQL

```
SELECT *
 FROM customers
ORDER BY name ASC;  -- Ascending order (A-Z)
```

2. `INSERT` **(Add data)**

The INSERT statement adds new rows to a table.

Basic syntax:

SQL

```
INSERT INTO table_name (column1, column2, ...)
VALUES (value1, value2, ...);
```

Example: Add a new customer to the customers table:

SQL

```
INSERT INTO customers (name, email, country)
    VALUES ('Jane    Doe',    'jane@example.com',
'Canada');
```

3. UPDATE **(Modify data)**

The UPDATE statement modifies existing data in a table.

Basic syntax:

SQL

```
UPDATE table_name
SET column1 = value1, column2 = value2, ...
WHERE condition;
```

Example: Update the email address of a customer with customer_id 1:

SQL

```
UPDATE customers
SET email = 'janedoe@email.com'
WHERE customer_id = 1;
```

4. DELETE (Remove data)

The DELETE statement removes rows from a table.

Basic syntax:

SQL

```
DELETE FROM table_name
WHERE condition;
```

Example: Delete a customer with customer_id 1:

SQL

```
DELETE FROM customers
WHERE customer_id = 1;
```

Important Notes:

Case sensitivity: SQL keywords are not case-sensitive (e.g., SELECT is the same as select), but table and column names might be, depending on your MySQL server's settings.

Semicolons: Use semicolons (;) to terminate SQL statements.

SQL Injection: Be mindful of SQL injection vulnerabilities when using user-provided data in your SQL queries. Always sanitize user input to prevent security risks.

These basic SQL commands are the foundation for interacting with your MySQL database. As you become more familiar with them, you can explore more advanced SQL features to perform complex queries and data manipulation.

3.4 Data modeling and database design

Data modeling and database design are crucial steps in building efficient and reliable applications. They help you structure your data effectively and ensure that your database can handle your application's needs.

Data Modeling

Data modeling is the process of creating a visual representation of the data your application will use. This representation helps you understand the relationships between different data elements and how they will be stored in the database.

Common Data Models:

Relational Model: The most common model, where data is organized into tables with rows and columns. Relationships are established between tables through foreign keys.

Entity-Relationship Diagram (ERD): A visual representation of the relational model, using entities (tables), attributes (columns), and relationships to depict the data structure.

Other Models: Hierarchical, network, object-oriented, and NoSQL models exist, each with its own approach to data organization.

Steps in Data Modeling:

1 Requirements Gathering: Understand the data needs of your application. What data will be stored? How will it be used?

2 Conceptual Modeling: Create a high-level overview of the data structure, often using an ERD to represent entities and relationships.

3 Logical Modeling: Refine the conceptual model, defining data types, constraints, and validation rules.

4 Physical Modeling: Translate the logical model into a specific database schema, considering the features and limitations of the chosen database system (e.g., MySQL).

Database Design

Database design is the process of applying the data model to create a database schema. This involves:

Creating Tables: Define the tables needed to store the data, including column names, data types, and constraints (e.g., primary keys, foreign keys, unique constraints).

Defining Relationships: Establish relationships between tables using foreign keys to ensure data integrity and avoid redundancy.

Normalization: Apply normalization techniques to reduce data redundancy and improve data integrity.

Optimization: Consider performance implications and optimize the database design for efficient data retrieval and manipulation.

Key Considerations in Database Design:

Data Integrity: Ensure data accuracy and consistency through constraints, validation rules, and referential integrity.

Performance: Design the database for efficient data retrieval and manipulation, considering indexing, query optimization, and data normalization.

Scalability: Plan for future growth and ensure the database can handle increasing amounts of data and user traffic.

Security: Implement security measures to protect sensitive data from unauthorized access.

Tools for Data Modeling and Database Design:

MySQL Workbench: Provides tools for visual data modeling, creating ERDs, and generating SQL scripts for database creation.

DbSchema: A visual database designer that supports multiple database systems.

Lucidchart: A diagramming tool that can be used to create ERDs and other data models.

By carefully planning your data model and database design, you can create a solid foundation for your application, ensuring data integrity, performance, and scalability.

Chapter 4

Working with MySQL Databases in PHP

4.1 Connecting to MySQL using PHP.

You're ready to start interacting with your MySQL database from your PHP applications! Here's how to establish that connection:

1. Choose your extension:

PHP offers two main extensions for connecting to MySQL:

MySQLi (Improved MySQL): The newer and recommended extension. It provides an object-oriented interface, as well as a procedural one, and supports features like prepared statements (important for security).

PDO (PHP Data Objects): A database abstraction layer that can be used with various database systems, not just MySQL. It offers a consistent API and helps prevent SQL injection.

2. MySQLi (Object-oriented approach)

PHP

```php
<?php
$servername   =   "localhost";        //   Usually
"localhost" for a local server
$username   =   "your_username";   //   Your   MySQL
username
$password   =   "your_password";   //   Your   MySQL
password
$dbname = "your_database"; // The   name   of   your
database
```

```php
// Create connection
$conn   =   new   mysqli($servername,   $username,
$password, $dbname);

// Check connection
if ($conn->connect_error) {
        die("Connection      failed:      "      .
$conn->connect_error);[1]
}
 echo "Connected successfully";[2]
 ?>
```

3. MySQLi (Procedural approach)

PHP

```php
<?php
$servername = "localhost";
$username = "your_username";
$password = "your_password";
$dbname = "your_database";

// Create connection
$conn   =   mysqli_connect($servername,   $username,
$password, $dbname);

// Check connection
if (!$conn) {
        die("Connection[3]      failed:      "      .
mysqli_connect_error());
}
echo "Connected successfully";[4]
?>
```

4. PDO

PHP

```php
<?php
$servername = "localhost";
$username = "your_username";
$password = "your_password";
$dbname = "your_database";

try {
    $conn = new
PDO("mysql:host=$servername;dbname=$dbname",
$username, $password);5
  // Set the PDO error mode to exception
        $conn->setAttribute(PDO::ATTR_ERRMODE,
PDO::ERRMODE_EXCEPTION);
  echo "Connected successfully";
} catch(PDOException $e) {
  echo "Connection failed: " . $e->getMessage();6
}
?>
```

Explanation:

Credentials: Replace "your_username", "your_password", and "your_database" with your actual MySQL credentials.

Error handling: It's essential to check for connection errors. The code examples show how to display an error message if the connection fails.

Closing the connection: When you're finished with your database operations, it's good practice to close the connection using `$conn->close();` (MySQLi) or by setting `$conn = null;` (PDO).

Choosing an approach:

MySQLi (Object-oriented): Generally preferred for its cleaner syntax and better organization, especially in larger projects.

MySQLi (Procedural): Might be simpler for very basic scripts.

PDO: A good choice if you might need to work with different database systems in the future or if you want to take advantage of its more advanced features.

No matter which approach you choose, make sure you have the correct MySQL credentials and that your MySQL server is running. Once connected, you can start executing SQL queries to interact with your database!

4.2 Executing SQL queries with PHP.

Once you've connected to your MySQL database using PHP, you can start executing SQL queries to retrieve, add, update, or delete data. Here's how to do it using both MySQLi and PDO:

MySQLi (Object-oriented)

PHP

```php
<?php
// ... (your connection code from the previous
example) ...

// SQL query
$sql = "SELECT * FROM customers";

// Execute query
$result = $conn->query($sql);
```

```php
// Check if any rows were returned
if ($result->num_rows > 0) {
  // Output data of each row
  while($row = $result->fetch_assoc()) {
    echo[1] "Name: " . $row["name"]. " - Email: " .
$row["email"]. "<br>";
  }
} else {
  echo "0 results";[2]
}

// Close connection
$conn->close();
?>
```

MySQLi (Procedural)

PHP

```php
<?php
// ... (your connection code) ...

// SQL query
$sql = "SELECT * FROM customers";

// Execute query
$result = mysqli_query($conn, $sql);

// Check if any rows were returned
if (mysqli_num_rows($result) > 0) {
  // Output data of each row
  while($row = mysqli_fetch_assoc($result))[3] {
    echo "Name: " . $row["name"]. " - Email: " .
$row["email"]. "<br>";
```

```php
  }
} else {
  echo "0 results";[4]
}

// Close connection
mysqli_close($conn);
?>
```

PDO

PHP

```php
<?php
// ... (your connection code) ...

// SQL query
$sql = "SELECT * FROM customers";

// Execute query and fetch results
foreach ($conn->query($sql) as $row) {
   echo "Name: " . $row["name"]. " - Email: " .
$row["email"]. "<br>";
}

// Or, fetch all results into an array
$stmt = $conn->query($sql);
$results = $stmt->fetchAll(PDO::FETCH_ASSOC);

// Close connection (optional with PDO, as it
closes automatically)
$conn = null;
?>
```

Explanation

`$sql`: This variable holds your SQL query as a string.

`$conn->query($sql)`: This executes the SQL query on the database.

`$result`: This variable stores the result of the query. It's a result set object in MySQLi and a PDOStatement object in PDO.

`fetch_assoc()`: This method fetches a row from the result set as an associative array (where keys are column names).

Looping through results: You typically use a `while` loop to iterate through the rows returned by the query.

Error handling: For production code, you should always include error handling to catch potential issues with your queries (e.g., invalid SQL syntax).

Important considerations

Prepared statements: For security and performance, especially when dealing with user input, use prepared statements to prevent SQL injection vulnerabilities.

Different query types: The `query()` method is used for `SELECT` queries. For queries that don't return result sets (like `INSERT`, `UPDATE`, `DELETE`), use `$conn->exec($sql)` in MySQLi or `$conn->prepare($sql); $stmt->execute();` in PDO.

By combining your knowledge of SQL queries with these PHP techniques, you can start building dynamic web applications that interact with your MySQL database!

4.3 Fetching and displaying data.

Fetching data from a MySQL database using PHP involves executing a `SELECT` query and then processing the results. Here's how to fetch and display data using both MySQLi and PDO:

1. MySQLi (Object-oriented)

PHP

```php
<?php
// ... (your connection code) ...

// SQL query
$sql = "SELECT * FROM products";
$result = $conn->query($sql);

if ($result->num_rows > 0) {
  echo "<ul>"; // Start an unordered list
  while($row = $result->fetch_assoc()) {
    echo "<li>";
     echo "<b>" . $row["product_name"] . "</b> -
$" . $row["price"];
    echo "</li>";
  }
  echo "</ul>"; // Close the list
} else {
  echo "No products found.";
}

$conn->close();
?>
```

2. MySQLi (Procedural)

PHP

```php
<?php
// ... (your connection code) ...

// SQL query
```

```php
$sql = "SELECT * FROM products";
 $result = mysqli_query($conn, $sql);

if (mysqli_num_rows($result) > 0) {
  echo "<ol>"; // Start an ordered list
  while($row = mysqli_fetch_assoc($result)) {
    echo "<li>";
     echo $row["product_name"] . " (Category: " .
$row["category"] . ")";
    echo "</li>";
  }
  echo "</ol>"; // Close the list
} else {
  echo "No products found.";
}

mysqli_close($conn);
?>
```

3. PDO

PHP

```php
<?php
// ... (your connection code) ...

// SQL query
$sql = "SELECT * FROM products";
 $stmt = $conn->query($sql);

echo "<table>"; // Start a table
echo                              "<tr><th>Product
Name</th><th>Price</th></tr>";
while ($row = $stmt->fetch(PDO::FETCH_ASSOC)) {
  echo "<tr>";
```

```php
      echo     "<td>"    .     $row["product_name"]     .
"</td><td>$" . $row["price"] . "</td>";
  echo "</tr>";
}
echo "</table>"; // Close the table

// Close connection (optional with PDO)
$conn = null;
?>
```

Explanation

`fetch_assoc()`: This method fetches a row from the result set as an associative array, where the keys are the column names.

Looping through results: The `while` loop iterates through each row returned by the query.

Displaying data: Inside the loop, you can access the data from each row using the column names as keys (e.g., `$row["product_name"]`).

HTML formatting: The examples use HTML tags (`<ul>`, `<li>`, `<b>`, etc.) to format the output. You can customize this to fit your needs.

Important points

Error handling: Always include error handling in production code to catch potential issues with your queries.

Security: Be mindful of potential SQL injection vulnerabilities when displaying data that might come from user input. Sanitize any user-provided data before using it in your queries.

Data presentation: Consider how you want to present the data to the user. You can use tables, lists, divs, or any other HTML elements to structure your output.

By combining your SQL knowledge with these PHP techniques, you can effectively retrieve and display data from your MySQL database in your web applications!

4.4 Handling database errors.

You're absolutely right to be thinking about error handling! It's a crucial part of writing robust and reliable database interactions in PHP. Here's how to handle database errors effectively using MySQLi and PDO:

MySQLi

Procedural approach:

PHP

```php
<?php
// ... (your connection code) ...

$sql = "SELECT * FROM customer"; // Intentional typo in table name

$result = mysqli_query($conn, $sql);

if (!$result) {
  echo "Error: " . mysqli_error($conn);
  // You might also want to log the error or take other actions
  // exit; // Stop further execution if needed
} else {
  // ... process the results ...
}

mysqli_close($conn);
?>
```

Object-oriented approach:

PHP

```php
<?php
// ... (your connection code) ...

$sql = "INSERT INTO customers (name, email)
VALUES ('Test', 'test@example')"; // Missing .com

if ($conn->query($sql) === TRUE) {
  echo "New record created successfully";
} else {
  echo "Error: " . $conn->error;
}

$conn->close();
?>
```

PDO

PDO offers a more sophisticated approach to error handling using exceptions:

PHP

```php
<?php
// ... (your connection code) ...

try {
```

```php
    $sql = "UPDATE customers SET email =
'new@email' WHERE id = 1"; // Syntax error
    $conn->exec($sql);
    echo "Record updated successfully";
} catch(PDOException $e) {
    echo "Error: " . $e->getMessage();
}

$conn = null;
?>
```

Explanation

`mysqli_error($conn)` / `$conn->error`: These functions return a string describing the error that occurred during the last MySQLi operation.

`$e->getMessage()`: This method (in PDO) returns the error message associated with the caught exception.

Error checking: Always check the return value of functions like `mysqli_query()` or `$conn->query()`. They will return `false` on failure.

`try...catch` **blocks (PDO):** This structure allows you to gracefully handle exceptions that might be thrown during database operations.

Error logging: In a production environment, it's essential to log database errors to a file or error tracking system so you can investigate and fix issues.

Best practices

Be specific: Catch specific exception types (in PDO) to handle different errors differently.

Don't expose sensitive information: Avoid displaying raw error messages to users, as they might contain sensitive information about your database.

Provide user-friendly feedback: If an error occurs, display a generic error message to the user and log the details for debugging.

Use transactions: For operations that involve multiple queries, use transactions to ensure data consistency. If one query fails, the entire transaction can be rolled back.

By implementing proper error handling, you can make your PHP database interactions more robust, prevent unexpected behavior, and improve the overall user experience of your applications.

Chapter 5

Building Dynamic Web Pages

5.1 Handling user input with forms

Handling user input from forms is a fundamental aspect of web development with PHP. Here's a breakdown of the process:

1. Create the HTML form

HTML

```
<form method="post" action="process.php">
  <label for="name">Name:</label><br>
          <input        type="text"        id="name"
name="name"><br><br>
  <label for="email">Email:</label><br>
          <input     type="email"     id="email"
name="email"><br><br>[1]
  <input type="submit" value="Submit">[2]
</form>
```

`method="post"`: Specifies that the form data will be sent using the HTTP POST method (more secure for sensitive data than GET).

`action="process.php"`: Specifies the PHP file that will process the form data.

`name` **attribute:** Each input field needs a `name` attribute. This is how you'll access the submitted values in your PHP code.

2. Process the form data in PHP (`process.php`)

PHP

```php
<?php
if ($_SERVER["REQUEST_METHOD"] == "POST") {
  // Access form data using $_POST superglobal
  $name = $_POST["name"];
  $email = $_POST["email"];

  // Validate the data (important for security!)
  // ... (validation code - see below) ...

  // Sanitize the data (important for security!)
  // ... (sanitization code - see below) ...

  // Now you can use the sanitized data to:
  // - Display it back to the user
  // - Store it in a database
  // - Send an email
  // - Perform other actions

  echo "<h2>Thank you for your submission!</h2>";
  echo "<p>Name: " . $name . "</p>";
  echo "<p>Email: " . $email . "</p>";
}
?>
```

3. Data validation

Why validate? To ensure data integrity and security.

Common validation checks:

Required fields

Data types (e.g., email, number)

Data format (e.g., date, phone number)

Data length

Example:

PHP

```php
if (empty($_POST["name"])) {
  $nameErr = "Name is required";
} else {
  $name = $_POST["name"];
}
```

4. Data sanitization

Why sanitize? To prevent security vulnerabilities like cross-site scripting (XSS).

Common sanitization techniques:

`htmlspecialchars()` - Converts special characters to HTML entities.

`trim()` - Removes whitespace from the beginning and end of a string.

`stripslashes()` - Removes backslashes.

Example:

PHP

```php
$name = htmlspecialchars($_POST["name"]);
```

Important considerations

Security: Always validate and sanitize user input to prevent security risks.

Error handling: Display helpful error messages to the user if validation fails.

User experience: Provide clear instructions and feedback to the user during the form submission process.

By following these steps, you can effectively handle user input from forms, process the data securely, and use it to create dynamic and interactive web applications.

5.2 Processing and validating data.

Processing and validating data received from user input is crucial for ensuring data integrity, security, and the overall reliability of your web application. Here's a breakdown of the process:

1. Accessing User Input

$_POST **Superglobal:** When a form is submitted with method="post", the form data is available in the $_POST superglobal array. You access individual values using their name attributes as keys:

PHP

```php
$name = $_POST["name"];
$email = $_POST["email"];
```

2. Data Validation

Purpose: To ensure that the data entered by the user meets the requirements of your application.

Common Validation Checks:

Required Fields: Check if mandatory fields have been filled out.

Data Types: Validate that the input matches the expected data type (e.g., email, number, date).

Data Format: Ensure the input follows a specific format (e.g., a valid email address, a phone number with the correct number of digits).

Data Length: Check if the input falls within acceptable length limits.

Numeric Ranges: Validate that numbers fall within a specified range.

Pattern Matching: Use regular expressions to validate complex patterns (e.g., passwords with specific character requirements).

3. Example Validation Code

PHP

```php
$name = $_POST["name"];
$email = $_POST["email"];
$errors = array(); // Array to store error messages

if (empty($name)) {
  $errors["name"] = "Name is required";
}

if (empty($email)) {
  $errors["email"] = "Email is required";
} elseif (!filter_var($email,
FILTER_VALIDATE_EMAIL)) {
  $errors["email"][1] = "Invalid email format";
}
```

```php
// If² there are errors, display them to the user
if (!empty($errors)) {
  foreach ($errors as $error) {
    echo "<p style='color: red;'>$error</p>";
  }
} else {
  // Proceed with processing the valid data
  // ...
}
```

4. Data Sanitization

Purpose: To remove or neutralize potentially harmful characters from user input, preventing security vulnerabilities like cross-site scripting (XSS).

Common Sanitization Techniques:

htmlspecialchars(): Converts special characters (like <, >, &, ") to their corresponding HTML entities, preventing them from being interpreted as HTML code.

trim(): Removes whitespace from the beginning and end of a string.

stripslashes(): Removes backslashes.

5. Example Sanitization Code

PHP

```php
$name = htmlspecialchars($_POST["name"]);
$email         =           filter_var($_POST["email"],
FILTER_SANITIZE_EMAIL);
```

6. Processing Valid Data

Once the data is validated and sanitized, you can proceed with processing it:

Store in a Database: Use SQL queries (`INSERT`) to store the data in your MySQL database.

Display to the User: Show a confirmation message or display the submitted data back to the user.

Send an Email: Use PHP's mail functions to send an email containing the data.

Perform Other Actions: Use the data for any other logic required by your application.

Important Considerations

Security: Prioritize security by always validating and sanitizing user input.

User Experience: Provide clear and user-friendly error messages to guide the user in providing correct input.

Context-Aware Validation: Tailor your validation rules to the specific context of the data. For example, a password field might have different requirements than a comment field.

Regular Expressions: Learn and use regular expressions for more complex validation scenarios.

By carefully processing and validating user input, you can create more secure, reliable, and user-friendly web applications.

5.3 Displaying dynamic content.

Displaying dynamic content is where the real power of PHP and MySQL shines! It allows you to create web pages that change based on user interactions, data from your database, and other factors. Here's a breakdown of how to display dynamic content:

1. Fetch data from your database

Use a SELECT query to retrieve the data you want to display. You'll typically use MySQLi or PDO to execute the query and fetch the results.

PHP

```php
<?php
// ... (your database connection code) ...

$sql = "SELECT * FROM products WHERE category = 'electronics'";
$result = $conn->query($sql);
?>
```

2. Use PHP to generate HTML

Embed PHP code within your HTML to dynamically generate the content. You can use loops, conditional statements, and variables to control what is displayed.

PHP

```php
<?php
if ($result->num_rows > 0) {
  echo "<ul>";
  while($row = $result->fetch_assoc()) {
    echo "<li>";
    echo "<h3>" . $row["product_name"] . "</h3>";
    echo "<p>" . $row["description"] . "</p>";
    echo "<p>Price: $" . $row["price"] . "</p>";
    echo "</li>";
  }
  echo "</ul>";
```

```php
} else {
    echo "<p>No products found in this
category.</p>";
}

$conn->close();
?>
```

3. Combine data with HTML

Use PHP to insert data from your database directly into your HTML.

PHP

```php
<h1>Welcome, <?php echo $_SESSION["username"];
?>!</h1>
<p>Your last login was on: <?php echo
$_SESSION["last_login"]; ?></p>
```

4. Conditional content

Use if statements to display different content based on conditions.

PHP

```php
<?php
if ($user_is_logged_in) {
  echo "<p>Welcome back!</p>";
  // Display user-specific content
} else {
  echo "<p>Please log in.</p>";
  // Display login form
```

```
}
?>
```

5. Loops for repetitive content

Use `for` or `foreach` loops to display lists of items.

PHP

```php
<?php
$colors = array("red", "green", "blue");
echo "<ul>";
foreach ($colors as $color) {
  echo "<li>$color</li>";
}
echo "</ul>";
?>
```

Example: Dynamic product listing

PHP

```php
<!DOCTYPE html>
<html>
<head>
  <title>Product Listing</title>
</head>
<body>

<h1>Our Products</h1>

<?php
// ... (database connection code) ...
```

```php
$sql = "SELECT * FROM products";
$result = $conn->query($sql);

if ($result->num_rows > 0) {
  echo "<div class='product-grid'>";
  while($row = $result->fetch_assoc()) {
    echo "<div class='product'>";
      echo "<img src='" . $row["image_url"] . "'
alt='" . $row["product_name"] . "'>";
    echo "<h2>" . $row["product_name"] . "</h2>";
    echo "<p>" . $row["description"] . "</p>";
      echo "<p class='price'>$" . $row["price"] .
"</p>";
    echo "</div>";
  }
  echo "</div>";
} else {
  echo "<p>No products found.</p>";
}

$conn->close();
?>

</body>
</html>
```

This example fetches product data from a database and dynamically generates a grid of product listings.

By mastering these techniques, you can create engaging and personalized web experiences that respond to user actions and data changes in real-time.

5.4 Introduction to templating engines.

You're diving into a key concept for building maintainable and scalable web applications! Here's an introduction to templating engines in PHP:

What is a templating engine?

A templating engine is a tool that helps you separate the presentation layer (HTML) from the application logic (PHP) in your web applications. Instead of embedding PHP code directly within your HTML, you use a template engine to create templates with placeholders for dynamic content. The engine then takes these templates and combines them with data from your PHP code to generate the final HTML output.

Why use a templating engine?

Cleaner code: Separating presentation and logic makes your code more organized, readable, and easier to maintain.

Improved design: Designers can work on templates without having to deal with PHP code.

Reusability: Templates can be reused across different parts of your application.

Security: Templating engines often provide features to help prevent security vulnerabilities like cross-site scripting (XSS).

Performance: Some templating engines offer caching mechanisms to improve performance.

Popular PHP templating engines

Twig: A flexible, fast, and secure templating engine. It has a clear syntax and a large community.

Blade: The templating engine used in the Laravel framework. It's known for its simple and elegant syntax.

Smarty: A feature-rich and mature templating engine.

Plates: A native PHP templating engine that's fast and easy to use.

How templating engines work

Template creation: You create template files with placeholders for dynamic content. These placeholders use a specific syntax defined by the templating engine.

Code snippet

```
<!DOCTYPE html>
<html>
<head>
  <title>{{ title }}</title> </head>
<body>
  <h1>{{ heading }}</h1>
  <ul>
    {% for product in products %}
      <li>{{ product.name }} - ${{ product.price }}</li>
    {% endfor %}
  </ul>
</body>
</html>
```

Data rendering: In your PHP code, you pass data to the templating engine.

PHP

```
$data = [
    'title' => 'Product Listing',
    'heading' => 'Our Products',
    'products' => $products // Array of products
from database
];

$twig->render('product_listing.twig', $data);
```

Output generation: The templating engine takes the template and the data, replaces the placeholders with the actual values, and generates the final HTML output.

Key features

Variables: `{{ variable_name }}`

Control structures: `{% if condition %}` ... `{% endif %}`, `{% for item in items %}` ... `{% endfor %}`

Filters: `{{ name | upper }}` (converts the name to uppercase)

Inheritance: Create base templates and extend them in child templates.

Includes: Include other templates within a template.

Getting started

Choose an engine: Select a templating engine that fits your needs and project requirements.

Install: Install the engine using Composer or by downloading the library.

Read the documentation: Familiarize yourself with the engine's syntax and features.

Start templating! Create your templates and integrate them with your PHP code.

Templating engines can significantly improve the structure and maintainability of your web applications, especially as they grow in complexity.

Chapter 6

User Authentication and Session Management

6.1 Implementing user registration and login.

1. Database Setup

Create a `users` **table:** You'll need a database table to store user information. Here's an example schema:

SQL

```sql
CREATE TABLE users (
    id INT AUTO_INCREMENT PRIMARY KEY,
    username VARCHAR(255) UNIQUE NOT NULL,
    email VARCHAR(255) UNIQUE NOT NULL,
    password[1] VARCHAR(255) NOT NULL
);
```

2. Registration Form (register.php)

HTML

```html
<!DOCTYPE html>
<html>
<head>
  <title>Registration</title>
</head>
<body>

<h2>Register</h2>
```

```
<form                                            method="post"
action="register_process.php">
  <label² for="username">Username:</label><br>
        <input      type="text"      id="username"
name="username" required><br><br>

  <label for="email">Email:</label><br>
   <input type="email" id="email" name="email"
required><br><br>

  <label for="password">Password:</label><br>³
       <input     type="password"     id="password"
name="password" required><br><br>

  <input type="submit" value="Register">
</form>

</body>⁴
</html>
```

3. Registration Processing (register_process.php)

PHP

```php
<?php
// ... (database connection code) ...

if ($_SERVER["REQUEST_METHOD"] == "POST") {
  $username = $_POST["username"];
  $email = $_POST["email"];
  $password = $_POST["password"];

  // Validate and sanitize input (important!)
```

```php
    // ...

    // Hash the password (essential for security!)
    $hashed_password = password_hash($password,
PASSWORD_DEFAULT);

    // SQL query to insert user data
    $sql = "INSERT INTO users (username, email,
password)
                VALUES ('$username', '$email',
'$hashed_password')";

    if ($conn->query($sql) === TRUE) {
      echo "Registration successful!";[5]
        // Redirect to login page or display a
success message
    } else {
        echo "Error: " . $sql . "<br>" .
$conn->error;
    }

    $conn->close();
}
?>
```

4. Login Form (login.php)

HTML

```html
<!DOCTYPE html>
<html>
<head>
    <title>Login</title>
</head>
<body>
```

```html
<h2>Login</h2>

<form method="post" action="login_process.php">
  <label for="username">Username:</label><br>[6]
        <input    type="text"    id="username"
name="username" required><br><br>

  <label for="password">Password:</label><br>
      <input    type="password"    id="password"
name="password" required><br><br>[7]

  <input type="submit" value="Login">[8]
</form>

</body>
</html>
```

5. Login Processing (login_process.php)

PHP

```php
<?php
// ... (database connection code) ...

if ($_SERVER["REQUEST_METHOD"] == "POST") {
  $username = $_POST["username"];
  $password = $_POST["password"];

  // Validate and sanitize input
  // ...

  // SQL query to fetch user data
```

```php
  $sql = "SELECT * FROM users WHERE username =
'$username'";
  $result = $conn->query($sql);

  if ($result->num_rows == 1) {
    $row = $result->fetch_assoc();
    // Verify the password
                if      (password_verify($password,
$row["password"]))[9] {
      echo "Login successful!";
        // Start a session, store user data in
session variables
      // Redirect to a protected page
    } else {
      echo "Incorrect password.";
    }
  } else {
    echo "Username not found.";
  }

  $conn->close();
}
?>
```

Key Considerations

Security:

Password hashing: Always hash passwords using `password_hash()` before storing them in the database.

Prepared statements: Use prepared statements to prevent SQL injection.

Input validation and sanitization: Validate and sanitize all user input to prevent XSS and other vulnerabilities.

Session management: Use sessions to keep track of logged-in users.

Error handling: Display appropriate error messages to the user.

User experience: Provide a clear and user-friendly registration and login process.

This is a basic implementation. For production systems, you'll want to add more features like email confirmation, password reset, and more robust security measures.

6.2 Hashing passwords securely.

You're spot on about the importance of secure password hashing! It's absolutely critical for protecting user accounts. Here's a breakdown of how to hash passwords securely in PHP:

1. Use `password_hash()`

PHP's built-in `password_hash()` function is the recommended way to hash passwords. It uses strong, one-way hashing algorithms (currently bcrypt by default) and automatically generates a random salt.

PHP

```
$password = $_POST["password"]; // Get the user's
password from the form
$hashed_password    =    password_hash($password,
PASSWORD_DEFAULT);
```

`PASSWORD_DEFAULT`**:** This uses the strongest algorithm currently supported by PHP (bcrypt).

Salt: A salt is a random string that's added to the password before hashing. This makes it much harder for attackers to crack passwords using techniques like rainbow tables. `password_hash()` handles salt generation automatically.

2. Store the hashed password

Store the `$hashed_password` in your `users` table in the database. Never store the plain text password!

3. Verify passwords with `password_verify()`

When a user tries to log in, use `password_verify()` to check the entered password against the stored hash.

PHP

```php
$entered_password = $_POST["password"]; //
Password entered by the user
$hashed_password = $row["password"]; // Hashed
password from the database

if            (password_verify($entered_password,
$hashed_password)) {
  // Passwords match! User is authenticated
} else {
  // Incorrect password
}
```

Why this is secure

One-way hashing: Hashing functions are designed to be one-way, meaning it's extremely difficult (computationally infeasible) to reverse the process and get the original password from the hash.

Salt: The use of a salt makes it much more difficult for attackers to use pre-computed tables (rainbow tables) to crack passwords.

Adaptive algorithms: `password_hash()` uses algorithms that are designed to be slow and computationally expensive, making it harder for attackers to use brute-force attacks.

Best practices

Use a strong algorithm: `PASSWORD_DEFAULT` will always use the strongest algorithm available in PHP.

Don't limit password length: Allow users to create long and complex passwords.

Encourage good password practices: Guide users in creating strong and unique passwords.

Protect your database: Secure your database server and access credentials to prevent unauthorized access.

Stay updated: Keep your PHP version and password hashing libraries up-to-date to benefit from the latest security improvements.

By following these guidelines, you can ensure that your users' passwords are hashed securely and protected from potential attacks.

6.3 Working with sessions.

Sessions are a vital mechanism in web development for maintaining user state and tracking information across multiple page requests. Since HTTP is a stateless protocol (each request is independent of the previous one), sessions provide a way to "remember" information about the user as they navigate your website.

Here's how sessions work in PHP:

1. Starting a Session

Before you can work with session variables, you need to start a session using `session_start()`. This function should be called at the beginning of your PHP script, before any output is sent to the browser.

PHP

```php
<?php
session_start();[1]
 ?>
```

2. Storing Session Variables

You can store data in session variables using the `$_SESSION` superglobal array.

PHP

```php
$_SESSION["username"] = "johndoe";
$_SESSION["email"] = "john@example.com";
$_SESSION["last_login"] = date("Y-m-d H:i:s");
```

3. Accessing Session Variables

You can access session variables on any page where the session is active.

PHP

```php
<?php
session_start();
```

```php
echo "Welcome, " . $_SESSION["username"] . "!";
?>
```

4. Modifying Session Variables

You can modify session variables just like regular variables.

PHP

```php
$_SESSION["username"] = "janedoe";
```

5. Deleting Session Variables

`unset()`: To delete a specific session variable:

PHP

```php
unset($_SESSION["username"]);
```

`session_destroy()`: To destroy the entire session and all session variables:

PHP

```php
session_destroy();
```

How Sessions Work Behind the Scenes

Session ID: When a session starts, a unique session ID is generated and typically stored in a cookie on the user's browser.

Session Data: The session data itself is usually stored on the server (in files or a database), associated with that session ID.

Session Management: With each request, the browser sends the session ID to the server. The server uses this ID to retrieve the corresponding session data and make it available to your PHP scripts.

Common Use Cases for Sessions

User Authentication: Storing user login information to track authenticated users.

Shopping Carts: Keeping track of items in a user's shopping cart as they browse an e-commerce site.

User Preferences: Storing user-specific settings and preferences.

Flash Messages: Displaying temporary messages to the user (e.g., success or error messages).

Important Considerations

Security: Protect session data from unauthorized access. Use HTTPS to secure the connection and regenerate session IDs periodically to prevent session hijacking.

Performance: Avoid storing large amounts of data in sessions, as this can impact performance.

Session Lifetime: Configure the session lifetime appropriately to balance security and user experience.

By understanding how sessions work, you can effectively use them to manage user state and create more dynamic and personalized web applications.

6.4 Protecting against common security threats (SQL injection, cross-site scripting).

You're thinking about security, which is excellent! SQL injection and cross-site scripting (XSS) are two of the most common and dangerous web application vulnerabilities. Here's how to protect against them in PHP:

SQL Injection

SQL injection occurs when attackers insert malicious SQL code into user input fields, tricking your application into executing unintended database queries. This can lead to data breaches, data modification, or even complete control of your database server.

Prevention techniques:

Prepared Statements: The most effective way to prevent SQL injection. Prepared statements separate SQL code from user data, ensuring that user input is treated as data, not as executable code.

PHP

```php
// MySQLi (object-oriented)
$stmt = $conn->prepare("SELECT * FROM users WHERE username = ?");
$stmt->bind_param("s", $username);
 $stmt->execute();

// PDO
$stmt = $conn->prepare("INSERT INTO products (name, price) VALUES (?, ?)");
$stmt->execute([$name, $price]);
```

Input Validation and Sanitization:

Validate: Check if the input matches the expected data type, format, and length.

Sanitize: Escape or remove potentially harmful characters.

PHP

```php
$username = htmlspecialchars($_POST["username"]);
// For text input
$id = (int)$_POST["id"];  // Type casting for integers
```

Stored Procedures: Encapsulate SQL logic within stored procedures on the database server. This can limit the attacker's ability to manipulate queries.

Least Privilege Principle: Grant database users only the necessary permissions to perform their tasks.

Cross-Site Scripting (XSS)

XSS happens when attackers inject malicious scripts into web pages viewed by other users. These scripts can steal cookies, hijack sessions, redirect users to malicious sites, or deface websites.

Prevention techniques:

Output Encoding: Escape special characters in output that might be interpreted as HTML or JavaScript code. Use `htmlspecialchars()` to encode data before displaying it.

PHP

```php
echo htmlspecialchars($comment);
```

Input Sanitization: Sanitize user input to remove or neutralize potentially harmful scripts.

Content Security Policy (CSP): A security header that helps reduce XSS risks by defining which sources of content are allowed to be loaded on a page.

HttpOnly Cookies: Set the `HttpOnly` flag on cookies to prevent them from being accessed by JavaScript.

General Security Best Practices

Keep Software Updated: Update your PHP version, MySQL server, and any libraries or frameworks you use to patch security vulnerabilities.

Secure Your Server: Configure your web server (Apache, Nginx) securely and use HTTPS to encrypt communication between the browser and the server.

Principle of Least Privilege: Grant users and processes only the minimum necessary permissions.

Regular Security Audits: Conduct regular security audits and penetration testing to identify and address vulnerabilities.[1]

By implementing these security measures, you can significantly reduce the risk of SQL injection and XSS vulnerabilities in your PHP applications.

Chapter 7

Building Efficient Applications

7.1 Optimizing database queries

Optimizing database queries is crucial for building fast and efficient applications. Slow queries can lead to poor user experience, increased server load, and higher costs. Here's a breakdown of techniques to optimize your MySQL queries:

1. Use Indexes

What are indexes? Indexes are like lookups in a book. They help the database find data quickly without scanning the entire table.

When to use them: Create indexes on columns frequently used in `WHERE` clauses, `JOIN` conditions, and `ORDER BY` clauses.

Example:

SQL

```
CREATE    INDEX    idx_lastname    ON    customers
(lastname);
```

Types of indexes: MySQL supports various index types (B-tree, hash, full-text) depending on your data and query patterns.

2. Select Only What You Need

Avoid `SELECT *`: Specify the columns you need instead of retrieving all columns. This reduces data transfer and processing time.

Example:

SQL

```
SELECT name, email
 FROM customers;
```

3. Optimize JOINs

Choose the right JOIN **type:** Use INNER JOIN, LEFT JOIN, RIGHT JOIN appropriately based on your needs.

Join on indexed columns: Ensure that the columns used in JOIN conditions are indexed.

Reduce the number of JOINs**:** If possible, restructure your queries to minimize the number of joins.

4. Limit the Data Retrieved

LIMIT **clause:** Use LIMIT to retrieve only the necessary number of rows.

Pagination: Implement pagination to display large datasets in smaller chunks.

5. Avoid WHERE **clauses on indexed columns**

Functions on indexed columns: Avoid using functions on indexed columns in WHERE clauses, as this can prevent the index from being used.

SQL

```
// Inefficient:
```

```
SELECT     *     FROM     products     WHERE
YEAR(release_date) = 2023;
```

```
// Efficient:
SELECT * FROM products WHERE release_date
BETWEEN '2023-01-01' AND '2023-12-31';
```

6. Optimize `LIKE` clauses

Wildcard placement: When using `LIKE`, place wildcards (`%`) at the end of the pattern whenever possible.

SQL

```
// Efficient:
SELECT * FROM customers WHERE lastname LIKE
'Smith%';
```

```
// Inefficient:
SELECT * FROM customers WHERE lastname LIKE
'%Smith%';
```

7. Use `EXISTS` instead of `IN` (sometimes)

`EXISTS` **for subqueries:** `EXISTS` can be more efficient than `IN` when checking for the existence of a record in a subquery.

8. Analyze Query Performance

`EXPLAIN` **statement:** Use `EXPLAIN` to see how MySQL executes your query and identify potential bottlenecks.

Slow query log: Enable MySQL's slow query log to track queries that take longer than a specified threshold.

Profiling tools: Use profiling tools to get detailed information about query execution time.

9. Keep Your Data Normalized

Database normalization: Properly normalize your database schema to reduce data redundancy and improve query performance.

10. Choose the Right Data Types

Efficient data types: Use the most efficient data types for your columns (e.g., `INT` instead of `VARCHAR` for integers).

By applying these optimization techniques, you can significantly improve the performance of your database queries and create faster, more efficient applications.

7.2 Caching techniques

Caching is a powerful technique for improving the performance and scalability of web applications. It involves storing frequently accessed data in a temporary storage location (the cache) so that it can be retrieved faster in subsequent requests. Here's a breakdown of caching techniques you can use in your PHP and MySQL applications:

1. Output Caching (Page Caching)

How it works: Store the entire HTML output of a page in the cache. When the same page is requested again, serve the cached version directly, bypassing the PHP execution and database queries.

Good for: Static pages or pages with content that doesn't change frequently.

Implementation:

PHP's ob_start() **and** ob_get_contents(): Capture the output buffer and store it in the cache.

Caching libraries: Use libraries like Zend Cache or Symfony Cache component.

Example:

PHP

```php
<?php
// Check if the page is cached
if        ($cached_content        =
get_from_cache('my_page')) {
  echo $cached_content;
  exit;
}


// If not cached, generate the page content
ob_start();
// ... your PHP code to generate the page
content ...
$content = ob_get_contents();
```

```php
ob_end_clean();

// Store the content in the cache
store_in_cache('my_page', $content);

// Output the content
echo $content;
?>
```

2. Fragment Caching

How it works: Cache specific parts or fragments of a page. This is useful when only certain sections of a page are dynamic.

Good for: Pages with a mix of static and dynamic content (e.g., a product page with a static header and footer but dynamic product details).

Implementation:

Output buffering: Use `ob_start()` and `ob_get_contents()` to cache specific blocks of code.

Templating engines: Many templating engines (like Twig and Blade) have built-in support for fragment caching.

3. Data Caching

How it works: Cache the results of database queries or API calls. When the same query is executed again, retrieve the data from the cache instead of hitting the database or external service.

Good for: Data that is frequently accessed but doesn't change very often (e.g., product catalogs, user profiles).

Implementation:

Memcached or Redis: Use in-memory data stores like Memcached or Redis for fast data caching.

Caching libraries: Leverage caching libraries that provide an abstraction layer for different caching backends.

4. Object Caching

How it works: Cache entire objects or data structures (e.g., user objects, product objects) to avoid repeated object creation or database retrieval.

Good for: Complex objects that are expensive to create or retrieve.

Implementation:

Serialization: Serialize objects and store them in the cache.

Object-relational mapping (ORM) frameworks: Many ORM frameworks (like Doctrine or Eloquent) have built-in support for object caching.

5. Browser Caching

How it works: Leverage browser caching to store static assets (like images, CSS, and JavaScript files) on the user's browser.

Good for: Improving page load times and reducing server load.

Implementation:

HTTP headers: Use HTTP headers like `Cache-Control` and `Expires` to control how long assets should be cached by the browser.

Important Considerations

Cache Invalidation: Implement mechanisms to invalidate the cache when data changes.

Cache Size: Choose an appropriate cache size based on your server resources and application needs.

Cache Eviction Policies: Understand different cache eviction policies (e.g., LRU, LFU) to determine how items are removed from the cache when it's full.

By effectively implementing caching techniques, you can significantly improve the performance, scalability, and user experience of your PHP and MySQL applications.

7.3 Code optimization and profiling.

Code optimization and profiling are essential techniques for improving the performance and efficiency of your PHP applications. Let's break down each concept:

Code Optimization

Code optimization involves modifying your code to make it execute faster, use less memory, or consume fewer resources. Here are some common code optimization techniques in PHP:

Use efficient algorithms and data structures: Choose algorithms and data structures that are well-suited to the task at hand. For example, use a hash table (array in PHP) for fast lookups instead of searching through a list.

Minimize database queries: Reduce the number of database queries by fetching only the necessary data and using caching techniques.

Optimize loops: Avoid unnecessary computations within loops and use the most efficient looping constructs (e.g., `foreach` for arrays).

Avoid unnecessary object creation: Creating objects can be expensive. Reuse objects when possible and avoid creating temporary objects within loops.

Use built-in functions: PHP provides many optimized built-in functions. Use them instead of writing your own implementations whenever possible.

Optimize string manipulation: Use efficient string functions and avoid unnecessary string concatenation.

Reduce function calls: Function calls have overhead. Inline short functions or reduce the number of function calls if possible.

Use appropriate data types: Choose the most efficient data types for your variables (e.g., `int` instead of `string` for integers).

Enable opcode caching: Opcode caching (like OPcache) stores compiled PHP bytecode in memory, reducing the need to recompile code on each request.

Code Profiling

Code profiling is the process of analyzing your code's execution to identify performance bottlenecks. Profiling tools help you understand which parts of your code are consuming the most time or resources.

Popular PHP profiling tools:

Xdebug: A powerful debugging and profiling tool for PHP. It can generate detailed profiling information that can be visualized with tools like KCacheGrind or Webgrind.

Blackfire.io: A commercial profiling service that provides deep insights into code performance, including function call times, memory usage, and I/O operations.

Tideways: Another commercial profiling tool with features like performance monitoring, error tracking, and SQL analysis.

Steps in Code Profiling

1 Identify performance issues: Use performance testing or user feedback to identify areas of your application that are slow or inefficient.

2 Choose a profiling tool: Select a profiling tool that meets your needs and integrate it with your development environment.

3 Run the profiler: Execute your code with the profiler enabled to collect performance data.

4 Analyze the results: Use the profiling tool's reports to identify performance bottlenecks. Look for functions or code blocks that consume a significant amount of time or resources.

5 Optimize the code: Apply code optimization techniques to address the identified bottlenecks.

6 Repeat: Re-run the profiler to measure the impact of your optimizations and continue iterating until you achieve the desired performance improvements.

Benefits of Code Optimization and Profiling

Improved performance: Faster loading times and better user experience.

Reduced resource usage: Lower server costs and improved scalability.

Increased efficiency: More efficient use of hardware and software resources.

Better code quality: Cleaner, more maintainable, and more reliable code.

By combining code optimization techniques with code profiling tools, you can identify and address performance bottlenecks in your PHP applications, resulting in faster, more efficient, and more scalable code.

7.4 Scaling your application.

Scaling your application means ensuring it can handle increasing traffic, data volume, and user demands without compromising performance or stability. It's a critical aspect of building successful web applications, especially as your user base grows. Here's a breakdown of key concepts and techniques for scaling PHP and MySQL applications:

1. Vertical Scaling (Scaling Up)

How it works: Increase the resources of your existing server (e.g., more RAM, faster CPU, larger storage).

Pros: Simpler to implement, no code changes usually required.

Cons: Limited by the capacity of a single server, can be expensive, single point of failure.

2. Horizontal Scaling (Scaling Out)

How it works: Add more servers to distribute the load.

Pros: Higher scalability potential, better fault tolerance, more cost-effective in the long run.

Cons: More complex to implement, requires load balancing and potentially code changes.

3. Load Balancing

Purpose: Distribute incoming traffic across multiple servers to prevent overload on any single server.

Load balancers: Hardware or software that acts as a reverse proxy, directing requests to different servers based on factors like server load, location, etc.

Popular load balancers: Nginx, HAProxy, Amazon Elastic Load Balancing.

4. Database Scaling

Scaling MySQL:

Read replicas: Create read-only copies of your database to handle read-heavy workloads.

Sharding: Partition your database across multiple servers to distribute data and query load.

Caching: Cache frequently accessed data to reduce database load.

NoSQL databases: Consider using NoSQL databases (like MongoDB or Cassandra) for specific data needs that are better suited to their architecture.

5. Caching

Purpose: Store frequently accessed data in a cache (e.g., Memcached, Redis) to reduce database and processing load.

Types of caching: Output caching, fragment caching, data caching, object caching.

6. Code Optimization

Efficient code: Write optimized code that minimizes resource usage and execution time.

Profiling: Use profiling tools (like Xdebug) to identify and address performance bottlenecks.

7. Asynchronous Processing

How it works: Offload time-consuming tasks (e.g., sending emails, processing images) to background processes or queues to avoid blocking the main application thread.

Tools: Gearman, RabbitMQ, Beanstalkd.

8. Content Delivery Network (CDN)

Purpose: Distribute static assets (images, CSS, JavaScript) across multiple servers geographically closer to users.

Benefits: Faster page load times, reduced server load.

9. Cloud Computing

Cloud platforms: AWS, Google Cloud, Azure.

Benefits: Scalability, reliability, pay-as-you-go pricing.

10. Monitoring and Performance Tuning

Monitoring tools: New Relic, Datadog, Prometheus.

Track key metrics: CPU usage, memory usage, database performance, response times.

Important Considerations

Application architecture: Design your application with scalability in mind from the start.

Statelessness: Make your application as stateless as possible to facilitate horizontal scaling.

Session management: Use a centralized session storage (e.g., Redis) when scaling horizontally.

Scaling is an ongoing process that requires careful planning, monitoring, and optimization. By understanding these techniques and applying them strategically, you can build robust and scalable PHP and MySQL applications that can handle growth and meet user demands.

Chapter 8

Security Best Practices

8.1 Input validation and sanitization.

Why Input Validation and Sanitization Matter

Prevent Security Vulnerabilities: Failing to validate and sanitize user input can open your application to various attacks, including:

SQL Injection: Attackers inject malicious SQL code into input fields to manipulate your database.

Cross-Site Scripting (XSS): Attackers inject malicious scripts into web pages viewed by other users.

Cross-Site Request Forgery (CSRF): Attackers trick users into performing unwanted actions on your website.

Command Injection: Attackers execute system commands on your server.

Ensure Data Integrity: Validation ensures that the data entered by users meets your application's requirements, preventing errors and inconsistencies.

Improve User Experience: Clear validation feedback helps users provide correct input, leading to a smoother user experience.

Input Validation

Input validation is the process of checking whether the data entered by the user conforms to the expected format, type, and range.

Common Validation Techniques

Required Fields: Check if mandatory fields have been filled out.

Data Types: Verify that the input is of the correct data type (e.g., integer, string, email).

Data Format: Ensure the input follows a specific format (e.g., a valid email address, a date in YYYY-MM-DD format).

Data Length: Check if the input falls within acceptable length limits.

Numeric Ranges: Validate that numbers fall within a specified rango.

Pattern Matching: Use regular expressions to validate complex patterns (e.g., passwords with specific character requirements).

Example Validation Code

PHP

```php
$name = $_POST["name"];
$email = $_POST["email"];
$age = $_POST["age"];
$errors = array();

if (empty($name)) {
  $errors["name"] = "Name is required";
}

if (empty($email)) {
  $errors["email"] = "Email is required";
} elseif (!filter_var($email, FILTER_VALIDATE_EMAIL)) {
```

```php
        $errors["email"][1]  =   "Invalid   email
format";
    }


    if[2] (!is_numeric($age) || $age < 0 || $age >
    120) {

        $errors["age"] = "Age must be a number
between 0 and 120";

    }


    if (!empty($errors)) {
      // Display errors to the user
    } else {
      // Proceed with processing the valid data
    }
```

Input Sanitization

Input sanitization is the process of cleaning or transforming user input to remove or neutralize potentially harmful characters or code.

Common Sanitization Techniques

`htmlspecialchars()`: Converts special characters (like <, >, &, ") to their corresponding HTML entities, preventing them from being interpreted as HTML code.

`trim()`: Removes whitespace from the beginning and end of a string.

`stripslashes()`: Removes backslashes.

Database-specific escaping: Use functions like `mysqli_real_escape_string()` (MySQLi) or parameterized queries (PDO) to escape special characters that could interfere with SQL queries.

Example Sanitization Code

PHP

```php
$name = htmlspecialchars($_POST["name"]);
$comment = htmlspecialchars($_POST["comment"]);


// Using MySQLi
$username = mysqli_real_escape_string($conn, $_POST["username"]);


// Using PDO (preferred)
$stmt = $conn->prepare("INSERT INTO comments (user_id, comment) VALUES (?, ?)");
$stmt->execute([$user_id, $comment]);
```

Important Considerations

Validate First, Sanitize Second: Always validate input before sanitizing it. This ensures that you're working with valid data before applying sanitization techniques.

Context-Aware Sanitization: Use sanitization methods that are appropriate for the context in which the data will be used. For example, if you're displaying user input on a web page, use `htmlspecialchars()`. If you're storing it in a database, use database-specific escaping or parameterized queries.

Defense in Depth: Combine multiple layers of defense (validation, sanitization, prepared statements) to provide comprehensive protection against attacks.

By diligently implementing input validation and sanitization, you can create more secure and reliable PHP applications that are protected from common web vulnerabilities.

8.2 Preventing SQL injection and cross-site scripting (XSS).

You're focusing on two of the most critical web application security risks! Preventing SQL injection and cross-site scripting (XSS) is essential to protect your data and your users. Here's a breakdown of how to prevent these vulnerabilities in PHP:

Preventing SQL Injection

SQL injection occurs when attackers insert malicious SQL code into user input fields, which can allow them to manipulate your database.

Key Prevention Techniques

Prepared Statements: This is the **most effective** method. Prepared statements separate SQL code from user data, ensuring that user input is treated as data, not executable code.

PHP

```php
// MySQLi (object-oriented)
$stmt = $conn->prepare("SELECT * FROM users
WHERE username = ? AND password = ?");
```

```
$stmt->bind_param("ss",                $username,
$password);

$stmt->execute();


// PDO

$stmt = $conn->prepare("INSERT INTO products
(name, price) VALUES (?, ?)");

$stmt->execute([$name, $price]);
```

Input Validation and Sanitization:

Validate: Check if the input matches the expected data type, format, and length.

Sanitize: Escape or remove potentially harmful characters using functions like `mysqli_real_escape_string()` (MySQLi).

PHP

```
$id = (int)$_POST["id"]; // Type casting for
integers

$username = mysqli_real_escape_string($conn,
$_POST["username"]); // Escaping for MySQLi
```

Stored Procedures: Encapsulate SQL logic within stored procedures on the database server. This can limit the attacker's ability to manipulate queries directly.

Least Privilege Principle: Grant database users only the necessary permissions to perform their tasks.

Preventing Cross-Site Scripting (XSS)

XSS happens when attackers inject malicious scripts into web pages viewed by other users. These scripts can then steal data, hijack sessions, or redirect users to malicious sites.

Key Prevention Techniques

Output Encoding: Escape special characters in output that might be interpreted as HTML or JavaScript code. Use `htmlspecialchars()` to encode data before displaying it.

PHP

```php
echo htmlspecialchars($comment);
```

Input Sanitization: Sanitize user input to remove or neutralize potentially harmful scripts. You can use a combination of:

`htmlspecialchars()`

`strip_tags()` (with allowed tags if needed)

Custom functions or libraries to remove or escape specific patterns.

Content Security Policy (CSP): A security header that helps reduce XSS risks by defining which sources of content are allowed to be loaded on a page.

HttpOnly Cookies: Set the `HttpOnly` flag on cookies to prevent them from being accessed by JavaScript. This helps protect against session hijacking.

General Security Best Practices

Keep Software Updated: Update your PHP version, MySQL server, and any libraries or frameworks you use to patch security vulnerabilities.

Secure Your Server: Configure your web server (Apache, Nginx) securely and use HTTPS to encrypt communication between the browser and the server.

Principle of Least Privilege: Grant users and processes only the minimum necessary permissions.

Regular Security Audits: Conduct regular security audits and penetration testing to identify and address vulnerabilities[1] proactively.

By diligently implementing these security measures, you can significantly reduce the risk of SQL injection and XSS vulnerabilities in your PHP applications, protecting both your data and your users.

8.3 Protecting against cross-site request forgery (CSRF).

Understanding CSRF

CSRF attacks exploit the trust that a website has in a user's browser. Here's a typical scenario:

1 User Login: A user logs into your website, and their browser stores a session cookie (or other authentication token) that identifies them as logged in.

2 Malicious Website: The user visits a malicious website (or a legitimate website that has been compromised).

3 Hidden Request: The malicious website contains hidden code (e.g., an image tag with a malicious URL, a hidden form) that sends a request to your website.

4 Exploiting Trust: Since the user's browser automatically includes their session cookie with the request, your website thinks the request is coming from the legitimate user and processes it.

Example:

Imagine a malicious website with this code:

HTML

```
<img
src="https://yourwebsite.com/transfer_money?
amount=1000&to=attacker" />
```

If a logged-in user visits this malicious site, their browser will automatically send a request to your website to transfer money to the attacker's account, without the user's knowledge or consent.

Prevention Techniques

Synchronizer Token Pattern (STP)

How it works:

Generate a unique, unpredictable token for each user session.

Include this token as a hidden field in every form that performs a state-changing action (e.g., transferring money, changing passwords, deleting accounts).

When the form is submitted, verify that the token submitted with the request matches the token stored in the user's session.

Example:

PHP

```php
// Generate a token
$_SESSION['csrf_token'] = bin2hex(random_bytes(32));

// In your form
<input type="hidden" name="csrf_token" value="<?php echo $_SESSION['csrf_token']; ?>">

// When processing the form
if ($_POST['csrf_token'] !== $_SESSION['csrf_token']) {
    // Invalid token, reject the request
}
```

Double Submit Cookie

How it works:

Set a cookie with a random value.

Include the same value as a hidden field in the form.

When the form is submitted, verify that the value in the cookie matches the value in the form field.

SameSite Cookies

How it works:

Use the `SameSite` attribute for your session cookies. This attribute tells the browser to only send the cookie with requests originating from the same site, preventing cross-site requests from including the cookie.

`SameSite=Strict` provides the strongest protection but might affect legitimate cross-site interactions.

`SameSite=Lax` is a more relaxed option that allows some cross-site requests (like those from links) but blocks others (like those from forms embedded on other sites).

Other Techniques

Re-authentication: Require users to re-authenticate (e.g., enter their password) for sensitive actions.

CAPTCHA: Use CAPTCHAs to verify that the request is coming from a human.

Important Considerations

Token Security: Generate strong, unpredictable tokens and store them securely.

Token Validation: Always validate tokens before processing any sensitive requests.

HTTPS: Use HTTPS to encrypt communication between the browser and the server, preventing attackers from intercepting and modifying tokens.

By implementing these CSRF prevention techniques, you can significantly enhance the security of your PHP applications and protect your users from unauthorized actions.

8.4 Securely handling file uploads.

You're spot on with your concern about file uploads! They can be a significant security risk if not handled carefully. Here's a breakdown of how to securely handle file uploads in PHP:

1. Server-Side Validation

File Type Validation: Always validate the file type on the server-side. Don't rely solely on client-side validation, as it can be easily bypassed. Use functions like `mime_content_type()` or `finfo_file()` to determine the actual file type.

PHP

```php
$allowed_types = ['image/jpeg', 'image/png', 'image/gif'];

$file_type = mime_content_type($_FILES['file']['tmp_name']);

if (!in_array($file_type, $allowed_types)) {
    // Invalid file type, reject the upload
}
```

File Size Validation: Limit the maximum allowed file size to prevent denial-of-service attacks or excessive storage usage.

PHP

```php
$max_file_size = 5 * 1024 * 1024; // 5MB
if      ($_FILES['file']['size']        >
$max_file_size) {
    // File size exceeds the limit, reject
the upload
}
```

Other Validation: Consider validating other file attributes like dimensions (for images), file extensions, and content (e.g., checking for malicious code within the file).

2. Secure File Storage

Store Outside Web Root: Store uploaded files outside the web root directory to prevent direct access to them through the browser.

Unique Filenames: Generate unique filenames for uploaded files to avoid overwriting existing files and to make it harder for attackers to guess filenames.

PHP

```
$filename    =    uniqid()    .    '_'    .
basename($_FILES['file']['name']);

$target_dir = '/path/to/uploads/directory/';

 $target_file = $target_dir . $filename;
```

File Permissions: Set appropriate file permissions on the upload directory and uploaded files to restrict access.

3. Prevent Script Execution

Disable Script Execution: Configure your web server to prevent script execution in the upload directory. This can be done using `.htaccess` files (for Apache) or server configuration directives.

Filename Sanitization: Sanitize filenames to remove potentially dangerous characters or extensions that could allow script execution (e.g., `.php`, `.php3`).

4. Use a Secure Upload Mechanism

Avoid `move_uploaded_file()` **for sensitive files:** For very sensitive files, consider using more secure methods like writing the file contents directly to a database or using a dedicated file storage service.

5. Additional Security Measures

Content Security Policy (CSP): Use CSP headers to restrict the types of resources that can be loaded on your website, reducing the risk of XSS attacks if a malicious file is somehow executed.

Input Validation and Sanitization: Always validate and sanitize any user input related to the file upload, such as filenames or descriptions.

Example Code

PHP

```php
<?php
$target_dir = "/path/to/uploads/directory/";
$target_file     =      $target_dir    .
basename($_FILES["file"]["name"]);
$uploadOk = 1;
$imageFileType                         =
strtolower(pathinfo($target_file,PATHINFO_EX
TENSION));[1]


// Check if image file is a actual image or
fake image
if(isset($_POST["submit"])) {
                        $check           =
getimagesize($_FILES["file"][[2]"tmp_name"]);
  if($check !== false) {
        echo  "File  is  an  image  -  "  .
$check["mime"] . ".";
    $uploadOk = 1;
  } else {
    echo "File is not an image.";
    $uploadOk = 0;
  }
}


// Check if file already exists
```

```php
if (file_exists($target_file)) {
  echo "Sorry, file already exists.";
  $uploadOk = 0;
}


// Check file size
if ($_FILES["file"]["size"]$^3$ > 500000) {
  echo "Sorry, your file is too large.";
  $uploadOk = 0;
}


// Allow certain file formats
if($imageFileType != "jpg" && $imageFileType
!= "png" && $imageFileType != "jpeg"
&& $imageFileType != "gif" ) {
   echo "Sorry, only JPG, JPEG, PNG & GIF
files are allowed.";
  $uploadOk = 0;
}


// Check if $uploadOk is set to 0 by an
error
if ($uploadOk == 0) {
  echo "Sorry, your file was not uploaded.";
// if everything is ok, try to upload file
} else {
```

```
                                             if
(move_uploaded_file($_FILES["file"]["tmp_nam
e"],⁴ $target_file)) {

        echo "The file ". htmlspecialchars(
basename( $_FILES["file"]["name"])). " has
been uploaded.";

   } else {

        echo "Sorry, there was an error
uploading your file.";⁵

   }

}

?>
```

By following these security practices, you can significantly reduce the risks associated with file uploads and protect your application from potential attacks.

Chapter 9

APIs and Web Services

9.1 Building RESTful APIs with PHP.

REST (Representational State Transfer) is a popular architectural style for building web services. RESTful APIs use standard HTTP methods (GET, POST, PUT, DELETE) to interact with resources, making them easy to understand and integrate with.

Here's how you can build RESTful APIs with PHP:

1. Define Your Resources

Identify the resources your API will expose. These are typically nouns representing the data your application manages (e.g., users, products, articles).

2. Design Your API Endpoints

Create API endpoints (URLs) that correspond to actions on your resources. Use HTTP methods to indicate the action:

`GET /users`: Retrieve a list of users.

`GET /users/{id}`: Retrieve a specific user by ID.

`POST /users`: Create a new user.

`PUT /users/{id}`: Update an existing user.[1]

`DELETE /users/{id}`: Delete[2] a user.

3. Handle API Requests

Use PHP to handle incoming API requests. Here's a basic example:

PHP

```php
<?php
header('Content-Type: application/json');


// Get the HTTP method and requested
resource
$method = $_SERVER['REQUEST_METHOD'];
$request                 =          explode('/',
trim($_SERVER['PATH_INFO'],'/'));
$input                                           =
json_decode(file_get_contents('php://input')
,true);


// Connect to the database[3]
// ...


// Route the request to the appropriate
handler
switch ($method) {
  case 'GET':
    // ... handle GET requests ...
    break;
  case 'POST':
    // ... handle POST requests ...
    break;
  case 'PUT':
    // ... handle PUT requests ...
```

```php
      break;
    case 'DELETE':
      // ... handle DELETE requests ...
      break;
    default:[4]
        http_response_code(405);  // Method Not
Allowed
      break;
}


// Close the database connection
// ...


// Example GET request handler
function handleGetRequest($request) {
    global $conn; // Assuming $conn is your
database connection


        if      (isset($request[0])     &&
is_numeric($request[0])) {
      // Get a specific user by ID
      $user_id = $request[0];
      $sql = "SELECT * FROM users WHERE id =
$user_id";
        // ... execute query and return user
data as JSON ...
    } else {
```

```php
    // Get all users

    $sql = "SELECT * FROM users";

        // ... execute query and return user
data as JSON ...

    }

}

?>
```

4. Return Responses in JSON Format

RESTful APIs typically use JSON (JavaScript Object Notation) to exchange data. Use PHP's `json_encode()` function to convert data to JSON format.

PHP

```php
$response = ['message' => 'User created
successfully', 'user_id' => $new_user_id];
echo json_encode($response);
```

5. Handle Errors Gracefully

Return appropriate HTTP status codes (e.g., 400 Bad Request, 404 Not Found, 500 Internal Server Error) and error messages in JSON format.

6. Consider Using a Framework

PHP frameworks like Laravel, Symfony, and Slim can simplify API development by providing features like:

Routing

Request handling

Response formatting

Middleware (for authentication, authorization, etc.)

Example using Slim Framework:

PHP

```php
<?php
use Psr\Http\Message\ResponseInterface as Response;
use Psr\Http\Message\ServerRequestInterface as Request;
use Slim\Factory\AppFactory;

require __DIR__ . '/vendor/autoload.php';

$app = AppFactory::create();

$app->get('/users', 5    function (Request $request, Response $response, $args) {
    // Fetch users from the database
    $users = // ... your database logic ...

    $response->getBody()->write(json_encode($users));

                                    return
    $response->withHeader('Content-Type', 'application/json');
```

```
});


$app->run();

?>
```

Key Considerations

Security: Implement authentication and authorization to protect your API.

Documentation: Provide clear and comprehensive API documentation.

Versioning: Version your API to manage changes and ensure backward compatibility.

Error Handling: Provide informative error messages and appropriate HTTP status codes.

By following these steps and best practices, you can build robust and well-designed RESTful APIs with PHP that are easy to use and integrate with.

9.2 Consuming APIs with PHP.

Consuming APIs (Application Programming Interfaces) allows you to access data and functionality from external services, enriching your PHP applications with external capabilities. Here's how to consume APIs using PHP:

1. Choose an API Client Library (Optional)

While you can use PHP's built-in functions like `file_get_contents()` and `curl` to make API requests, using an API client library can simplify the process and provide additional features. Popular options include:

Guzzle: A powerful and widely-used HTTP client library.

HTTPlug: An HTTP client abstraction layer that allows you to use different client implementations interchangeably.

2. Make an API Request

Use the appropriate HTTP method (GET, POST, PUT, DELETE) to make the API request. Include any required headers (e.g., API keys, authorization tokens) and request parameters.

Example using `file_get_contents()`:

PHP

```php
$api_url = 'https://api.example.com/data?param1=value1&param2=value2';

$api_key = 'YOUR_API_KEY';


$options = [
    'http' => [
        'header' => "X-API-Key: $api_key\r\n",
        'method' => 'GET'
    ]
];
$context = stream_context_create($options);
$response = file_get_contents($api_url, false, $context);

// Process the response
$data = json_decode($response, true);
```

```
// ...
```

Example using Guzzle:

PHP

```php
require 'vendor/autoload.php'; // If you're
using Composer


$client = new GuzzleHttp\Client();


$response      =      $client->request('GET',
'https://api.example.com/data', [
    'headers' => [
        'X-API-Key' => 'YOUR_API_KEY'
    ],
    'query' => [
        'param1' => 'value1',
        'param2' => 'value2'
    ]
]);


$data    =    json_decode($response->getBody(),
true);
// ...
```

3. Handle the API Response

API responses are typically in JSON or XML format. Use PHP's `json_decode()` or `simplexml_load_string()` to parse the response and access the data.

4. Error Handling

Implement error handling to gracefully handle API errors (e.g., invalid requests, server errors). Check the HTTP status code and any error messages returned by the API.

5. Security Considerations

API Keys: Store your API keys securely and avoid exposing them in client-side code.

Authentication: Use appropriate authentication mechanisms (e.g., OAuth 2.0) if required by the API.

Rate Limiting: Be mindful of API rate limits to avoid being blocked.

Input Validation: Validate any data you send to the API to ensure it meets the API's requirements.

Example with Error Handling

PHP

```php
$api_url = 'https://api.example.com/data';


try {

        $response = $client->request('GET',
$api_url);


        if ($response->getStatusCode() == 200) {
```

```php
                                      $data     =
json_decode($response->getBody(), true);

        // ... process the data ...

    } else {

        // Handle API error

        echo "API request failed with status
code: " . $response->getStatusCode();

    }

}                                              catch
(GuzzleHttp\Exception\RequestException $e) {

        // Handle request exceptions (e.g.,
network errors)

        echo "API request failed: " .
$e->getMessage();

}
```

By following these steps and best practices, you can effectively consume APIs in your PHP applications, expanding their functionality and accessing a wealth of external data and services.

9.3 Introduction to JSON and XML.

JSON (JavaScript Object Notation)

What it is: A lightweight data-interchange format that is easy for humans to read and write and easy for machines to parse and generate.[1]

Structure: Uses a simple text-based format with key-value pairs and nested objects and arrays.

Example:

JSON

```
{
  "name": "John Doe",
  "age": 30,
  "city": "New York",
  "address": {
    "street": "123 Main St",
    "zip": "10001"
  },
      "interests":    ["reading",   "coding",
  "traveling"]
}
```

Common uses:

Web APIs: Exchanging data between web servers and clients.

Configuration files: Storing application settings.

Data storage: Storing data in NoSQL databases or files.

XML (Extensible Markup Language)

What it is: A markup language that defines a set of rules for encoding documents in a format that is both human-readable and machine-readable.[2]

Structure: Uses tags to define elements and attributes to provide additional information about elements.

Example:

XML

```xml
<person>
  <name>John Doe</name>
  <age>30</age>
  <city>New York</city>
  <address>
    <street>123 Main St</street>
    <zip>10001</zip>
  </address>
  <interests>
    <interest>reading</interest>
    <interest>coding</interest>
    <interest>traveling</interest>
  </interests>
</person>
```

Common uses:

Web services: Exchanging data between applications.

Data exchange: Sharing data between different systems.

Document formatting: Defining the structure and layout of documents (e.g., HTML, DocBook).

Key Differences

Feature	JSON	XML
Syntax	Simpler, uses braces, brackets, and colons	More verbose, uses tags and attributes
Data types	Supports basic data types (string, number, boolean, null, object, array)	Can represent more complex data structures
Readability	Generally easier to read	Can be more verbose and less readable
Parsing	Usually faster to parse	Can be slower to parse
Size	Typically smaller file size	Can have larger file size

Choosing Between JSON and XML

Simplicity and Performance: If you need a simple and lightweight format with good performance, JSON is often the preferred choice.

Complex Data Structures: If you need to represent more complex data structures or require features like metadata and namespaces, XML might be a better fit.

Existing Standards: Consider existing standards and conventions in your domain or industry.

Working with JSON and XML in PHP

PHP provides built-in functions for working with JSON and XML:

JSON:

`json_encode($data)`: Converts a PHP array or object to a JSON string.

`json_decode($jsonString, true)`: Parses a JSON string and returns a PHP array (with `true` as the second argument).

XML:

`simplexml_load_string($xmlString)`: Parses an XML string and returns a SimpleXMLElement object.

DOMDocument: Provides a more powerful API for manipulating XML documents.

By understanding JSON and XML, you can effectively exchange data between your PHP applications and other systems or services.

Chapter 10

Building a Content Management System

10.1 Designing the database schema.

Designing a database schema is a crucial step in building any application, and it's especially important for content management systems (CMS). A well-designed schema ensures data integrity, efficiency, and scalability. Here's a breakdown of the process, keeping in mind the specific needs of a CMS:

1. Identify the Core Entities

A CMS typically revolves around these core entities:

Users: Store user information (ID, username, email, password, roles, etc.).

Content: Store the actual content (ID, title, body, author, creation date, publication status, etc.).

Categories: Organize content into categories (ID, name, description, parent category).

Tags: Allow tagging of content with keywords (ID, name).

Comments: Store user comments on content (ID, content ID, user ID, comment text, date).

Media: Store images, videos, and other media files (ID, filename, type, size, upload date).

2. Define Table Structures

Create tables for each entity, defining columns and their data types:

users **table:**

SQL

```
CREATE TABLE users (
    id INT AUTO_INCREMENT PRIMARY KEY,
    username VARCHAR(255) UNIQUE NOT NULL,
    email VARCHAR(255) UNIQUE NOT NULL,
    password[1] VARCHAR(255) NOT NULL,
    role ENUM('admin', 'editor', 'author', 'subscriber') NOT NULL
);
```

content **table:**

SQL

```
CREATE TABLE content (
    id INT AUTO_INCREMENT PRIMARY KEY,
    title VARCHAR(255) NOT NULL,
    body TEXT,
    author_id INT,
    category_id INT,
    created_at TIMESTAMP DEFAULT CURRENT_TIMESTAMP,
    published_at TIMESTAMP NULL,
    status ENUM('draft', 'published', 'archived') NOT NULL,
```

```
        FOREIGN  KEY  (author_id)  REFERENCES
users(id),
        FOREIGN  KEY  (category_id) REFERENCES
categories(id)
);
```

categories **table:**

SQL

```
CREATE TABLE categories (
    id INT AUTO_INCREMENT PRIMARY KEY,
    name VARCHAR(255) NOT NULL,
    parent_id INT,
        FOREIGN  KEY  (parent_id)  REFERENCES
categories(id)²
);
```

tags **table:**

SQL

```
CREATE TABLE tags (
    id INT AUTO_INCREMENT PRIMARY KEY,
    name VARCHAR(255) UNIQUE NOT NULL
);
```

comments **table:**

SQL

```sql
CREATE TABLE comments (
    id INT AUTO_INCREMENT PRIMARY KEY,
    content_id INT NOT NULL,
    user_id INT NOT NULL,
    comment TEXT,
    created_at TIMESTAMP DEFAULT CURRENT_TIMESTAMP,
    FOREIGN KEY (content_id) REFERENCES content(id),
    FOREIGN KEY (user_id) REFERENCES users(id)
);
```

media **table:**

SQL

```sql
CREATE TABLE media (
    id INT AUTO_INCREMENT PRIMARY KEY,
    filename VARCHAR(255) NOT NULL,
    type VARCHAR(255) NOT NULL,
    size INT NOT NULL,
    uploaded_at TIMESTAMP DEFAULT CURRENT_TIMESTAMP
);
```

3. Establish Relationships

Define relationships between tables using foreign keys:

One-to-many: A user can create many content items (`users` to `content`).

Many-to-one: A content item belongs to one category (`content` to `categories`).

Many-to-many: A content item can have many tags, and a tag can be associated with many content items (requires a join table `content_tags`).

4. Consider Additional Features

Revision history: Store different versions of content.

Custom fields: Allow users to add custom fields to content.

Workflows: Implement content approval workflows.

SEO: Include fields for SEO metadata (title, description, keywords).

Plugins: Design a schema that can be extended by plugins.

5. Normalization

Apply normalization principles to reduce data redundancy and improve data integrity.

6. Optimization

Consider performance implications and optimize the schema with indexes and appropriate data types.

7. Tools

Use database design tools like MySQL Workbench or DbSchema to visualize and manage your schema.

Example: content_tags **join table**

SQL

```
CREATE TABLE content_tags (
    content_id INT NOT NULL,
    tag_id INT NOT NULL,
    PRIMARY KEY (content_id, tag_id),
        FOREIGN KEY (content_id) REFERENCES
content(id),
    FOREIGN KEY (tag_id) REFERENCES tags(id)
);
```

This allows you to associate multiple tags with a single content item and vice versa.

By carefully designing your database schema, you lay a solid foundation for your CMS, ensuring that it can efficiently manage content, users, and their interactions.

10.2 Implementing CRUD operations.

CRUD operations are the foundation of data manipulation in web applications. They stand for **Create, Read, Update, and Delete**, representing the four basic functions you need to interact with data in a database. Here's how to implement CRUD operations in PHP, typically using MySQL as the database:

1. Create (Insert data)

SQL INSERT **statement:** Use the INSERT statement to add new records to a table.

PHP Example (using MySQLi):

PHP

```php
<?php
// ... (database connection code) ...

$name = $_POST["name"];
$email = $_POST["email"];

// Sanitize input (important!)
// ...

$sql = "INSERT INTO users (name, email) VALUES (?, ?)";
$stmt = $conn->prepare($sql);
$stmt->bind_param("ss", $name, $email);

if ($stmt->execute()) {
  echo "New record created successfully";
} else {
    echo "Error:[1] " . $sql . "<br>" . $conn->error;
}

$stmt->close();
$conn->close();
?>
```

2. Read (Retrieve data)

SQL SELECT **statement:** Use the SELECT statement to retrieve data from a table.

PHP Example (using PDO):

PHP

```php
<?php
// ... (database connection code) ...


$sql = "SELECT * FROM products";
$stmt = $conn->query($sql);


$products =
$stmt->fetchAll(PDO::FETCH_ASSOC);


// Display the products
foreach ($products as $product) {
    echo $product['name'] . " - $" .
$product['price'] . "<br>";
}


$conn = null;
?>
```

3. Update (Modify data)

SQL UPDATE **statement:** Use the UPDATE statement to modify existing records.

PHP Example (using MySQLi):

PHP

```php
<?php
// ... (database connection code) ...

$id = $_POST["id"];
$new_name = $_POST["name"];

// Sanitize input
// ...

$sql = "UPDATE products SET name=? WHERE id=?";
$stmt = $conn->prepare($sql);
$stmt->bind_param("si", $new_name, $id);

if ($stmt->execute()) {
  echo "Record updated successfully";
} else {
    echo "Error updating record: " . $conn->error;
}
```

```php
$stmt->close();
$conn->close();
?>
```

4. Delete (Remove data)

SQL DELETE statement: Use the DELETE statement to delete records from a table.

PHP Example (using PDO):

PHP

```php
<?php
// ... (database connection code) ...

$id = $_POST["id"];

$sql = "DELETE FROM users WHERE id = :id";
$stmt = $conn->prepare($sql);
$stmt->bindParam(':id',                    $id,
PDO::PARAM_INT);

if ($stmt->execute()) {
  echo "Record deleted successfully";
} else {
    echo  "Error  deleting  record:  "  .
$stmt->errorInfo()[2];
}
```

```
$conn = null;

?>
```

Important Considerations

Security: Always sanitize user input to prevent SQL injection vulnerabilities. Use prepared statements or parameterized queries whenever possible.

Error Handling: Implement proper error handling to catch and handle potential database errors.

User Experience: Provide feedback to the user about the success or failure of CRUD operations.

Transactions: For operations that involve multiple queries (e.g., transferring money between accounts), use transactions to ensure data consistency.

By implementing CRUD operations securely and efficiently, you can create dynamic web applications that allow users to interact with your data in a meaningful way.

10.3 User roles and permissions

User roles and permissions are essential for controlling access and managing users within a system, especially in a CMS where you might have different types of users with varying levels of authority. Here's how to implement user roles and permissions:

1. Define User Roles

Identify Roles: Determine the different roles within your CMS (e.g., administrator, editor, author, contributor, subscriber).

Assign Permissions: Define the specific permissions associated with each role. For example:

Administrator: Full access to all features and content.

Editor: Can create, edit, and publish content, manage categories, and moderate comments.

Author: Can create and edit their own content.

Contributor: Can submit content for review but cannot publish it.

Subscriber: Can only view published content.

2. Database Design

users **Table:** Include a role column in your users table to store the user's role. You can use an ENUM or a separate roles table with a foreign key relationship.

SQL

```
CREATE TABLE users (
    id INT AUTO_INCREMENT PRIMARY KEY,
    username VARCHAR(255) UNIQUE NOT NULL,
    // ... other user fields ...
    role ENUM('admin', 'editor', 'author',
'contributor', 'subscriber') NOT NULL
);
```

permissions **Table (Optional):** If you have a more complex permission system, create a permissions table to store individual permissions and a role_permissions table to associate permissions with roles.

3. Implementation in PHP

Authentication: After a user logs in, retrieve their role from the database and store it in a session variable.

Authorization: Before allowing a user to perform an action, check if their role has the necessary permission.

PHP

```php
<?php
session_start();

// ... (database connection code) ...

// Example: Check if the user is an admin
if ($_SESSION['user_role'] == 'admin') {
  // Allow access to admin functionality
}

// Example: Check if the user can edit
content
if   (hasPermission($_SESSION['user_role'],
'edit_content')) {
  // Allow content editing
}

function hasPermission($role, $permission) {
```

```php
    // Query the database or use a cached
permission matrix
    // to check if the role has the given
permission
    // ...
}
?>
```

4. User Interface (UI) Considerations

Role-based UI: Show or hide UI elements (buttons, menus, forms) based on the user's role.

Clear Feedback: Provide clear feedback to the user if they try to access something they don't have permission for.

5. Best Practices

Principle of Least Privilege: Grant users only the permissions they need to perform their tasks.

Role Hierarchy: Consider implementing a role hierarchy (e.g., admin > editor > author) to simplify permission management.

Centralized Permission Management: Create a centralized system for managing roles and permissions.

Code Reusability: Create reusable functions or classes to handle authorization checks.

Example with a separate roles **table:**

SQL

```sql
CREATE TABLE roles (
    id INT AUTO_INCREMENT PRIMARY KEY,
```

```
        name VARCHAR(255) UNIQUE NOT NULL

    );


CREATE TABLE user_roles (

    user_id INT NOT NULL,

    role_id INT NOT NULL,

    PRIMARY KEY (user_id, role_id),

        FOREIGN  KEY  (user_id)  REFERENCES
    users(id),

        FOREIGN[1]  KEY  (role id)  REFERENCES
    roles(id)[2]

    );
```

This allows users to have multiple roles and provides more flexibility in managing permissions.

By implementing user roles and permissions effectively, you can enhance the security and usability of your CMS, ensuring that users have appropriate access to content and functionality.

10.4 Content publishing and management.

Content publishing and management is at the heart of any CMS. Here's how to implement these features, focusing on key aspects and considerations:

1. Content Creation

User Interface (UI): Provide a user-friendly interface for creating content. This typically involves:

Rich Text Editor: A WYSIWYG editor (like TinyMCE or CKEditor) allows users to format text, insert images, and create links.

Input Fields: Fields for title, body text, excerpt, author, categories, tags, and other metadata.

Media Uploads: Ability to upload and manage images, videos, and other media files.

Content Types: Support different content types (e.g., articles, pages, blog posts, custom post types).

Workflows: Implement workflows for content creation, review, and approval (e.g., draft, pending review, published).

2. Content Storage

Database: Store content data in a database (like MySQL). Use appropriate data types (e.g., `TEXT` or `MEDIUMTEXT` for the content body).

Revision History: Store different versions of content to allow for rollbacks and tracking changes.

Media Storage: Store media files in a secure location (outside the web root) and associate them with content entries.

3. Content Organization

Categories and Tags: Allow users to categorize and tag content for easy organization and retrieval.

Menus and Navigation: Provide tools for creating menus and navigation structures to help users find content.

Search: Implement a search functionality to allow users to find content by keywords or filters.

4. Content Publishing

Publication Status: Allow users to control the publication status of content (e.g., draft, published, scheduled).

Scheduling: Enable scheduling of content to be published at a specific date and time.

Content Previews: Provide a preview functionality for users to see how the content will look when published.

5. Content Management

Content Listing: Display a list of content items with filtering and sorting options.

Content Editing: Provide an interface for editing existing content.

Content Deletion: Allow users to delete content (with appropriate safeguards).

Content Archiving: Implement an archiving feature to move old content out of the main content area.

6. Security Considerations

User Roles and Permissions: Control access to content based on user roles and permissions.

Input Validation and Sanitization: Prevent security vulnerabilities like SQL injection and XSS.

Media Security: Securely handle media uploads to prevent malicious file uploads.

7. Performance Optimization

Caching: Cache frequently accessed content to improve performance.

Database Optimization: Optimize database queries and schema for efficient content retrieval.

Example Code Snippet (Publishing Content)

PHP

```php
<?php
// ... (database connection code) ...

$title = $_POST["title"];
$body = $_POST["body"];
$status = $_POST["status"]; // 'draft' or 'published'
$published_at = ($status == 'published') ? date('Y-m-d H:i:s') : null;

$sql = "INSERT INTO content (title, body, published_at) VALUES (?, ?, ?)";
$stmt = $conn->prepare($sql);
$stmt->bind_param("sss", $title, $body, $published_at);

if ($stmt->execute()) {
  echo "Content published successfully!";
} else {
    echo "Error: " . $sql . "<br>" . $conn->error;
}
```

```php
$stmt->close();

$conn->close();

?>
```

By combining these features and best practices, you can create a robust and user-friendly CMS that empowers users to effectively create, manage, and publish content.

Chapter 11

Building an E-commerce Application

11.1 Product catalog and shopping cart.

1. Database Design

products **table:**

SQL

```sql
CREATE TABLE products (
    id INT AUTO_INCREMENT PRIMARY KEY,
    name VARCHAR(255) NOT NULL,
    description TEXT,
    price DECIMAL(10,[1] 2) NOT NULL,
    image_url VARCHAR(255),[2]
    category_id INT,
        FOREIGN KEY (category_id) REFERENCES categories(id)
);
```

categories **table:**

SQL

```sql
CREATE TABLE categories (
    id INT AUTO_INCREMENT PRIMARY KEY,
    name VARCHAR(255) NOT NULL
```

```
);
```

cart **table:**

SQL

```sql
CREATE TABLE cart (
    id INT AUTO_INCREMENT PRIMARY KEY,
    user_id INT,
    product_id INT,
    quantity INT NOT NULL,
        FOREIGN KEY (user_id) REFERENCES
users(id),
        FOREIGN KEY (product_id) REFERENCES
products(id)[3]
);
```

2. Product Catalog

Displaying Products: Fetch products from the database and display them in a user-friendly format (grid, list, etc.).

PHP

```php
<?php
// ... (database connection code) ...

$sql = "SELECT * FROM products";
$result = $conn->query($sql);
```

```php
if ($result->num_rows > 0) {

    while($row = $result->fetch_assoc()) {

        // Display product information (name,
description, price, image)

        // ...

    }
} else {

    echo "No products found.";

}


$conn->close();

?>
```

Filtering and Sorting: Allow users to filter products by category, price range, etc., and sort by name, price, popularity.[4]

Search: Implement a search functionality to allow users to find products by keywords.

Pagination: If you have a large number of products, implement pagination to display them in smaller chunks.

3. Shopping Cart

Adding to Cart: When a user clicks "Add to Cart," add the product ID and quantity to the `cart` table (or use sessions for non-logged-in users).

PHP

```php
<?php
```

```php
session_start();

$product_id = $_POST["product_id"];
$quantity = $_POST["quantity"];

// Add to cart (using sessions)
$_SESSION['cart'][$product_id] = $quantity;

// Or, add to cart in the database for
logged-in users
// ...
?>
```

Viewing Cart: Display the contents of the cart, including product details, quantities, and total price.

Updating Cart: Allow users to update product quantities or remove items from the cart.

Checkout: Implement a checkout process to collect shipping and payment information and complete the order.[5]

4. Key Considerations

Session Management: Use sessions to store cart data for non-logged-in users.

Inventory Management: Keep track of product inventory and prevent overselling.

Security: Protect against vulnerabilities like SQL injection and CSRF.

User Experience: Provide a smooth and user-friendly shopping experience.

Example: Adding to Cart with AJAX

JavaScript

```javascript
// JavaScript (using jQuery)
$(document).ready(function() {

  $('.add-to-cart').click(function() {
                    var      product_id      =
$(this).data('product-id');

        var quantity = 1; // Or get quantity
from an input field


      $.ajax({

        type: 'POST',

        url: 'add_to_cart.php',

            data: { product_id: product_id,
quantity: quantity },

        success: function(response) {

            // Update cart display or show a
success message

          alert(response);

        }
      });
    });
  });
```

This code uses AJAX to add an item to the cart without requiring a page reload, providing a more seamless user experience.

By combining these features and best practices, you can create a robust and user-friendly e-commerce experience with a well-structured product catalog and a functional shopping cart.

11.2 Payment gateway integration.

Payment gateway integration is a crucial step in building any e-commerce application. It allows you to securely accept online payments from your customers. Here's a general guide to integrating a payment gateway into your PHP application:

1. Choose a Payment Gateway

Popular options: Stripe, PayPal, Paystack (popular in Africa), Flutterwave (popular in Africa), Square, Authorize.Net

Factors to consider:

Transaction fees

Supported payment methods (credit cards, debit cards, mobile wallets)

Security features

Integration options (API, hosted payment pages)

Customer support

2. Create a Merchant Account

Sign up for a merchant account with your chosen payment gateway provider. This will typically involve providing your business information and bank account details.

3. Obtain API Credentials

Once your merchant account is approved, you'll receive API credentials (API keys, secret keys, etc.) that you'll need to integrate with the payment gateway.

4. Choose an Integration Method

Direct API Integration: This gives you more control over the checkout process but requires more development effort. You'll use the payment gateway's API to handle payment processing directly within your application.

Hosted Payment Pages: This is a simpler option where the payment gateway provider hosts the checkout page. You redirect customers to the hosted page to complete the payment, and the provider handles the sensitive payment information.

5. Development and Integration

Server-Side Integration:

Use the payment gateway's API client library (if available) or make HTTP requests to their API endpoints.

Handle API responses and errors.

Implement security measures to protect sensitive data.

Client-Side Integration (if using direct API integration):

Use JavaScript to collect payment information and tokenize it using the payment gateway's client-side library.

Send the token to your server for processing.

6. Testing

Thoroughly test your payment gateway integration in a sandbox environment before going live. This allows you to simulate transactions without processing real payments.

7. Security Considerations

PCI DSS Compliance: If you handle sensitive payment information directly, ensure your application complies with the Payment Card Industry Data Security Standard (PCI DSS).

HTTPS: Always use HTTPS to encrypt communication between your application and the payment gateway.

Secure API Credentials: Store your API credentials securely and avoid exposing them in client-side code.

Prevent Fraud: Implement measures to prevent fraudulent transactions (e.g., address verification, CVV checks).

Example: Stripe Integration (Direct API Integration)

PHP

```php
require 'vendor/autoload.php'; // Assuming
you're using Composer and Stripe's PHP
library


\Stripe\Stripe::setApiKey('YOUR_STRIPE_SECRE
T_KEY');


try {
              $paymentIntent       =
\Stripe\PaymentIntent::create([
    'amount' => 1099, // Amount in cents
    'currency' => 'usd',
    // ... other payment details ...
```

```php
    ]);

    // Send the PaymentIntent client_secret to
your client-side code
        echo    json_encode(['clientSecret'    =>
$paymentIntent->client_secret]);

} catch (\Stripe\Exception\ApiErrorException
$e) {
    // Handle API errors
    http_response_code(500);
        echo    json_encode(['error'    =>
$e->getMessage()]);
}
```

This code creates a PaymentIntent on Stripe and sends the client_secret to your front-end, where you can use Stripe.js to complete the payment.

By carefully following the payment gateway provider's documentation and implementing best practices, you can securely integrate online payment processing into your PHP e-commerce application.

11.3 Order management and fulfillment.

Order management and fulfillment are critical processes in e-commerce, ensuring that customers receive their orders accurately and efficiently. Here's a breakdown of how to handle these aspects in your PHP e-commerce application:

1 Order Management

Order Placement

Capture Order Details: When a customer places an order, collect:

Customer information (name, address, email)

Shipping address

Billing address

Payment information (if not already processed)

Ordered items (product IDs, quantities)

Order total

Generate Order ID: Assign a unique order ID for tracking and reference.

Store Order Data: Store the order information in a database, typically in an `orders` table.

2 Order Processing

Payment Processing: If payment wasn't processed during checkout, process it now (using a payment gateway).

Inventory Management: Update inventory levels to reflect the ordered items.

Order Confirmation: Send an order confirmation email to the customer.

3 Order Tracking

Order Status: Update the order status (e.g., "Pending," "Processing," "Shipped," "Delivered").

Tracking Information: If applicable, provide tracking numbers and links to shipping carrier websites.

Order History: Allow customers to view their order history and track order status.

Order Fulfillment

1 Picking and Packing

Pick Items: Retrieve the ordered items from inventory.

Pack Items: Pack the items securely for shipping.

Generate Shipping Label: Create a shipping label with the customer's address and tracking information.

2 Shipping

Choose Shipping Method: Select a shipping carrier and service based on the customer's preferences and order details.

Ship the Order: Hand over the package to the shipping carrier.

Update Order Status: Update the order status to "Shipped" and provide tracking information.

3 Delivery

Delivery Confirmation: Track the delivery status and obtain confirmation of delivery.

Update Order Status: Update the order status to "Delivered."

4. Returns and Refunds

Return Requests: Provide a mechanism for customers to request returns or exchanges.

Process Returns: Process return requests and issue refunds or exchanges as needed.

Database Design

orders **table:**

SQL

```sql
CREATE TABLE orders (
    id INT AUTO_INCREMENT PRIMARY KEY,
    user_id INT,
    order_date TIMESTAMP DEFAULT CURRENT_TIMESTAMP,
    status ENUM('Pending', 'Processing', 'Shipped', 'Delivered', 'Cancelled') NOT NULL,
    shipping_address TEXT,
    billing_address TEXT,
    total_amount DECIMAL(10, 2) NOT NULL,
    FOREIGN KEY (user_id) REFERENCES users(id)
);
```

order_items **table:**

SQL

```sql
CREATE TABLE order_items (
    id INT AUTO_INCREMENT PRIMARY KEY,
    order_id INT NOT NULL,
    product_id INT NOT NULL,
    quantity INT NOT NULL,
    price DECIMAL(10, 2) NOT NULL,
```

```
        FOREIGN  KEY  (order_id)  REFERENCES
orders(id),

        FOREIGN  KEY  (product_id)  REFERENCES
products(id)

);
```

Key Considerations

Automation: Automate as much of the order management and fulfillment process as possible (e.g., email notifications, inventory updates).

Integration: Integrate with shipping carriers and payment gateways for a seamless experience.

Scalability: Design your system to handle increasing order volumes.

Customer Communication: Keep customers informed throughout the process with order updates and tracking information.

Example: Updating Order Status

PHP

```php
<?php
// ... (database connection code) ...

$order_id = $_POST["order_id"];

$new_status = $_POST["status"];  // e.g.,
'Shipped'

$sql = "UPDATE orders SET status=? WHERE
id=?";
```

```php
$stmt = $conn->prepare($sql);

$stmt->bind_param("si",              $new_status,
$order_id);


if ($stmt->execute()) {

  // Send shipping confirmation email to the
customer

  // ...

} else {

  // Handle error

}


$stmt->close();

$conn->close();

?>
```

By efficiently managing orders and streamlining fulfillment, you can ensure customer satisfaction and build a successful e-commerce business.

11.4 Security considerations for e-commerce.

Security is paramount for e-commerce, where you handle sensitive customer data and financial transactions. Here's a breakdown of key security considerations:

1. Secure Your Website

HTTPS: Use HTTPS to encrypt all communication between the browser and the server. This protects sensitive data (like login credentials and payment information) from interception. Obtain an SSL certificate from a trusted certificate authority (CA).

Web Application Firewall (WAF): A WAF helps protect against common web attacks like SQL injection, cross-site scripting (XSS), and cross-site request forgery (CSRF). Consider using a cloud-based WAF service or a WAF plugin for your web server.

Secure Hosting: Choose a reputable hosting provider that offers security features like firewalls, intrusion detection, and regular backups.

Content Security Policy (CSP): Implement CSP headers to control the resources the browser is allowed to load, reducing the risk of XSS attacks.

2. Protect Customer Data

Data Encryption: Encrypt sensitive customer data (like passwords, addresses, and payment information) both in transit and at rest. Use strong encryption algorithms and secure key management practices.

Access Control: Implement strict access controls to limit who can access customer data. Use role-based access control (RBAC) to grant permissions based on user roles.

Data Minimization: Collect only the customer data that is absolutely necessary.

Compliance: Comply with relevant data privacy regulations like GDPR and CCPA.

3. Secure Payment Processing

PCI DSS Compliance: If you handle credit card information directly, ensure your systems comply with the Payment Card Industry Data Security Standard (PCI DSS).

Payment Gateway Integration: Use a reputable payment gateway provider (like Stripe, PayPal, or Authorize.Net) to securely process payments.

Fraud Prevention: Implement fraud prevention measures like address verification, CVV checks, and 3D Secure.

4. Secure Authentication and Authorization

Strong Passwords: Enforce strong password policies and encourage users to use unique, complex passwords.

Multi-Factor Authentication (MFA): Implement MFA to add an extra layer of security to user accounts.

Session Management: Securely manage user sessions. Use HTTPS to protect session cookies, regenerate session IDs periodically, and implement appropriate session timeouts.

5. Regular Security Audits and Updates

Vulnerability Scanning: Regularly scan your website and applications for vulnerabilities.

Penetration Testing: Conduct periodic penetration testing to simulate real-world attacks and identify weaknesses.

Security Updates: Keep your software (PHP, MySQL, web server, CMS, plugins) up to date to patch security vulnerabilities.

Security Monitoring: Monitor your systems for suspicious activity and security breaches.

6. Other Considerations

Secure File Uploads: If your e-commerce application allows file uploads, implement secure file handling practices to prevent malicious file uploads.

Third-Party Integrations: Carefully evaluate the security of any third-party services or APIs you integrate with.

Security Awareness Training: Educate your employees about security best practices and common threats.

By implementing these security measures, you can create a secure e-commerce environment that protects your business and your customers.

Chapter 12

Next Steps and Further Learning

12.1 PHP frameworks (Laravel, Symfony).

You're diving into the world of streamlined PHP development! Laravel and Symfony are two of the most popular and powerful PHP frameworks. They provide a structured approach to building web applications, offering a wealth of features and tools to simplify development. Here's a breakdown:

What are PHP Frameworks?

Foundation: Frameworks provide a foundation and structure for your code, promoting organization and best practices.

Reusable Components: They offer reusable components and libraries for common tasks (e.g., database interaction, routing, templating, security).

Efficiency: Frameworks help you build applications faster by reducing repetitive coding.

Maintainability: They promote code maintainability by encouraging a structured approach and separation of concerns.

Laravel

Focus: Rapid development and ease of use. Known for its elegant syntax and developer-friendly features.

Key Features:

Eloquent ORM: A powerful object-relational mapper (ORM) for interacting with databases.

Blade Templating Engine: A simple and intuitive templating engine.

Artisan CLI: A command-line interface for common tasks (e.g., generating code, running database migrations).

Routing: A flexible routing system for defining API endpoints and web routes.

Authentication and Authorization: Built-in authentication and authorization features.

Testing: Tools and helpers for testing your application.

Symfony

Focus: Flexibility, scalability, and stability. Often used for complex and enterprise-level applications.

Key Features:

Reusable Components: A collection of reusable PHP components that can be used independently or as part of the framework.

Dependency Injection: A powerful technique for managing dependencies and promoting code reusability.

Security: Robust security features and best practices.

Performance: Optimized for performance and scalability.

Community: A large and active community providing support and resources.

Similarities

MVC Architecture: Both frameworks follow the Model-View-Controller (MVC) architectural pattern.

Open Source: Both are open-source and free to use.

Community Support: Both have large and active communities.

Differences

Feature	Laravel	Symfony
Learning Curve	Easier to learn, especially for beginners	Steeper learning curve, more complex
Development Speed	Faster development due to simplicity and built-in features	Can be slower due to more configuration and flexibility
Scalability	Scalable, but might require more effort for large applications	Highly scalable, designed for complex applications
Flexibility	Less flexible, more opinionated about how things should be done	More flexible, allows for customization and extension
Use Cases	Smaller to medium-sized projects, rapid prototyping	Large-scale applications, enterprise systems

Choosing a Framework

Project Complexity: For simpler projects, Laravel's ease of use might be preferable. For complex projects, Symfony's flexibility and scalability might be a better fit.

Development Speed: If rapid development is a priority, Laravel's built-in features can help you get started quickly.

Team Experience: Consider your team's experience and familiarity with the frameworks.

Getting Started

Installation: Both frameworks can be installed using Composer.

Documentation: Refer to the official documentation for each framework:

Laravel: laravel.com

Symfony: symfony.com

By leveraging the power of PHP frameworks like Laravel or Symfony, you can streamline your development process, build more maintainable applications, and focus on the unique aspects of your project.

12.2 Deployment and hosting.

Deployment is the process of taking your PHP application from your local development environment and making it live on the web for users to access. Hosting is providing the server infrastructure and resources to make your application accessible. Here's a breakdown of the key aspects:

1. Prepare Your Application

Finalize Code: Ensure your code is stable, tested, and ready for production.

Optimize Performance: Optimize your code, database queries, and assets (images, CSS, JavaScript) for performance.

Configure Environment: Set up environment variables for production settings (database credentials, API keys, etc.).

Dependency Management: Use a dependency manager like Composer to manage your project's dependencies.

Version Control: Use a version control system like Git to track changes and manage releases.

2. Choose a Hosting Provider

Shared Hosting: Affordable but limited resources and control. Suitable for small, low-traffic websites.

Virtual Private Server (VPS): More control and resources than shared hosting. Good for medium-traffic websites and applications.

Cloud Hosting: Highly scalable and reliable, with pay-as-you-go pricing. Suitable for applications with varying traffic demands.

Dedicated Server: Provides a dedicated physical server with maximum control and resources. Expensive but ideal for high-traffic, resource intensive applications.

Popular Hosting Providers

Cloud Hosting: AWS, Google Cloud, Azure, DigitalOcean, Linode

Shared/VPS Hosting: Bluehost, HostGator, SiteGround, A2 Hosting

Specialized PHP Hosting: Cloudways, Kinsta

3. Deployment Methods

Manual Deployment:

Upload files via FTP or SSH.

Configure the server environment.

Set up databases and dependencies.

Git-based Deployment:

Use Git to push code changes to the server.

Automate deployment with tools like Git Hooks or continuous integration/continuous delivery (CI/CD) pipelines.

Platform-Specific Tools:

Cloud providers often offer their own deployment tools and services (e.g., AWS Elastic Beanstalk, Google App Engine).

4. Server Configuration

Web Server: Configure a web server (Apache or Nginx) to serve your application.

PHP: Install and configure PHP on the server.

MySQL: Set up a MySQL database and import your database schema and data.

Domain Name: Point your domain name to your server's IP address using DNS records.

5. Post-Deployment

Testing: Thoroughly test your application in the production environment.

Monitoring: Monitor your application's performance and uptime.

Security: Implement security measures to protect your server and application from attacks.

Example: Deployment with Git

1 Initialize a Git repository: `git init`

2 Add your project files: `git add .`

3 Commit your changes: `git commit -m "Initial commit"`

4 Add a remote repository (e.g., on GitHub or GitLab): `git remote add origin <repository_url>`

5 Push your code to the remote repository: `git push -u origin main`

6 On the server, clone the repository: `git clone <repository_url>`

7 Set up a Git Hook (e.g., a post-receive hook) to automatically update the code on the server whenever you push changes.

Key Considerations

Scalability: Choose a hosting solution that can scale with your application's needs.

Security: Implement security best practices to protect your server and application.

Performance: Optimize your application and server configuration for performance.

Maintenance: Regularly update your software and perform server maintenance tasks.

By carefully planning your deployment and choosing the right hosting solution, you can ensure that your PHP application is accessible, reliable, and performs well for your users.

12.3 Keeping your skills up-to-date.

The tech world is constantly evolving, and for a PHP and MySQL developer, staying up-to-date is essential to remain competitive and build cutting-edge applications. Here's a breakdown of how to keep your skills sharp:

1. Embrace Continuous Learning

Never Stop Learning: Make learning a continuous process. The tech landscape changes rapidly, so dedicate time each week or month to learn new technologies and improve existing skills.

Stay Curious: Cultivate a curious mindset. Explore new tools, libraries, and frameworks. Don't be afraid to experiment and try things out.

2. Follow Industry Trends

Read Blogs and Publications: Stay informed about the latest trends, best practices, and emerging technologies by reading blogs, articles, and online publications (e.g., SitePoint, PHP.net, dev.to, CSS-Tricks).

Attend Conferences and Webinars: Attend conferences, workshops, and webinars to learn from experts, network with other developers, and discover new ideas.

Follow Influencers: Follow influential developers and thought leaders on social media and through their blogs.

3. Deepen Your PHP and MySQL Knowledge

Master Fundamentals: Solid fundamentals are crucial. Review and strengthen your understanding of core PHP concepts (OOP, data structures, algorithms) and MySQL (database design, query optimization).

Explore Advanced Topics: Dive deeper into advanced PHP features (e.g., generators, closures, asynchronous programming) and MySQL (e.g., stored procedures, triggers, performance tuning).

PHP Documentation: The official PHP documentation is an invaluable resource. Refer to it frequently to learn about new features and best practices.

4. Expand Your Skillset

Modern Frameworks: Learn popular PHP frameworks like Laravel, Symfony, or CodeIgniter. Frameworks provide structure, efficiency, and maintainability.

Frontend Technologies: Familiarize yourself with frontend technologies like HTML, CSS, JavaScript, and JavaScript frameworks (React, Vue, Angular) to build modern web applications.

DevOps: Learn about DevOps practices (version control, continuous integration/continuous delivery, automated testing) to improve your development workflow.

Security Best Practices: Stay updated on web security best practices to protect your applications from vulnerabilities.

5. Practice and Build Projects

Hands-on Experience: The best way to learn is by doing. Build real-world projects to apply your skills and gain experience.

Personal Projects: Work on personal projects that challenge you and allow you to explore new technologies.

Contribute to Open Source: Contribute to open-source projects to learn from experienced developers and give back to the community.

6. Engage with the Community

Online Communities: Participate in online communities like Stack Overflow, Reddit's r/PHP, and forums to ask questions, share knowledge, and learn from others.

Local Meetups: Attend local PHP meetups and user groups to connect with other developers in your area.

7. Stay Updated with PHP Versions

New Releases: Keep track of new PHP releases and their features. Upgrade your projects to take advantage of performance improvements, security updates, and new functionalities.

By actively engaging in these activities, you can ensure that your PHP and MySQL skills remain current, allowing you to build high-quality applications and thrive in the ever-evolving world of web development.

www.ingramcontent.com/pod-product-compliance
Lightning Source LLC
LaVergne TN
LVHW051734050326

832903LV00023B/918